Awakening to the Dream

Awakening to the Dream

Leo Hartong

NON-DUALITY PRESS

Awakening to the Dream
© Copyright 2001, Leo Hartong
© Copyright 2007, Non-Duality Press

To contact the author you can mail to:
author@awakeningtothedream.com

For more information visit:
www.awakeningtothedream.com

Published by: Non-Duality Press
6 Folkestone Road Salisbury SP2 8JP United Kingdom
www.non-dualitybooks.com

ISBN 10: 0-9547792-1-5
ISBN 13: 978-0-9547792-1-4

With Gratitude to:

Alan Watts for showing The Way of Zen;
Ramesh Balsekar, through whom Consciousness
Speaks;
Wayne Liquorman for removing the 'I' from the
understanding;
Tony Parsons for telling it As It Is;
Nathan Gill for taking the time to be clear;
Jae for invaluable tweaking, input and feedback;
Chuck Hillig for inspiring the title;
And the One who speaks through each and all.

O space and time! now I see it is true, what I guess'd at,
What I guess'd when I loaf'd on the grass,
What I guess'd while I lay alone in my bed,
And again as I walk'd the beach under the paling stars
*of the morning.**

---

* From *Song Of Myself* by Walt Whitman (1819 - 1892)

Contents

Foreword by Tony Parsons

The book, *Awakening to the Dream*, is written with a clarity of perception that is rare to find in the multitude of published outpourings that these days purport to express wisdom.

Most popular teachings about enlightenment are based on the mistaken idea that there is such a thing as a separate individual who can choose through effort and purification to attain something called enlightenment. This prescriptive and goal-orientated approach is, of course, very attractive to the guru mind, which above all else wishes to remain employed by simply compounding confusion. From the non-dualistic perception, however, no part of this activity is seen as relevant, and Leo Hartong speaks straight out of the clear blue sky of non-dualism, gently but uncompromisingly leading the readers to see the original and abiding nature of what they are.

The book begins very well, with a clear explanation of its intent, and throughout the work there is the feeling of reading a letter written by a friend who gently, but passionately, wants to make something very clear. As the writer communicates his perception of the mystery, he intersperses his ideas with appropriate traditional and contemporary quotations.

In simple terms, it is the absence of seeking that reveals the wonder of that which already is, but although this simple and awesome mystery is impossible to express in words, Leo's exploration is a joy to share in.

Tony Parsons   www.theopensecret.com

1

What happens when you fall off the earth's edge?

Is there a promise in awakening to what I truly am? Is there something I can get out of this that will improve my life? Will it make me a better and more successful person? In short: What will it be like to live an awakened life? These seem perfectly reasonable questions, and they frequently come up during the search.

For many, the hope for a better life is the core motivation to invest so heavily in this quest. There is, however, a problem with these questions that prevents a direct answer, and that is that they originate from the limited perspective the seeker wants to transcend. The questions may sound reasonable, but they are intrinsically flawed.

Let me give you a concrete example. Before we knew that the earth was round, the question of where one would end up after falling off its edge was perfectly reasonable. From our current perspective, however, the question makes no sense. If you were to go back in time, you could not provide a simple answer, but would have to explain that the earth is, in fact, round and falling off it is not possible. This, of course, would go against the common sense of the questioner, who would point to the horizon and insist that he could clearly see where the earth ended. Asking the questioner to imagine the perspective of an astronaut would probably be seen as a conceptual abstraction to avoid the real issue, namely: 'What happens when you fall off the earth's edge?' That being said, I'm going to tell you what you will get out of enlightenment. If the answer is initially disappointing, don't give up. Read on and see if you come to the place where disappointment changes into clarity.

So here we go: The answer is that you will get nothing out of it because enlightenment is the realization that there *is* no you to get enlightened; that your sense of separation and individuality is an illusion. This reply will most likely go against your direct experience. You might have learned that you are part of an ongoing process in which the fittest will survive and that you have to pass on your genes to the next generation or die trying. You may also believe that the art of living is in improving yourself and your life's circumstances. If you're poor and hungry, a roof over your head and a meal a day may do it for you. If you're lucky enough to live in a situation where your basic survival needs are covered, you will most likely pursue happiness and fulfillment via relationships, the acquisition of material goods, and social status.

When this is not enough you might become what is known as a seeker. A seeker is someone who feels that the so-called material world cannot deliver true and lasting contentment and that an inner dimension needs to be explored to find peace, enlightenment, or Self-realization. As a seeker you'll perhaps try psychotherapy, rebirthing, getting in touch with your inner child, past life regression therapy, yoga, transcendental meditation, or one of the other techniques believed to lead to lasting fulfillment and happiness. Such methods may indeed deliver results that you can experience as improving or enriching your life. However, you'll probably discover that after some time the original euphoria wears off. You come to realize that experiences and states of mind are always temporary. After this recognition, many seekers consider the so-called non-dual approach to Self-realization or enlightenment.

Non-duality is a general term that covers several – mostly eastern – schools of thought, which point to the single source before and beyond all temporal experiences and apparent diversity. While reading texts from non-dual systems such as Zen, Advaita, Taoism, or Dzogchen, you will find the affirmation that Self-realization has no promise other than to release you from your belief in a separate self or ego. That's it. The dropping away of an illusion simply revealing *this as it is*, often summed up in the phrase 'Before enlightenment chop wood and carry water. After enlightenment, chop wood and carry water.'

The ego, which certainly does not want to hear that it is an illusion, may claim to accept this as a concept, but invariably resists its realization, persisting in the belief that the carrying and chopping that come 'after' are somehow different. Now, if there's nothing in it for me, why would I even bother? 'Give me some motivation,' says the ego; 'Give me something that makes it worth my while to pursue this.'

This way of thinking seems right to us, who are conditioned to look for a future purpose in whatever it is we're doing. Logic dictates that we should gain something here instead of merely hearing that we don't exist. From this perspective, it gets even worse. Enlightenment not only shows that your separate identity is an illusion, it reveals that sheer purposelessness is at the heart of this whole creation. This sounds absurd to the goal-and-future-oriented mind; yet I will tell you unequivocally that the whole point of this manifestation is nothing other *than* this manifestation.

Realizing this is far from the bleak reality the mind imagines it to be. True, this is of no use to the ego, since it is about freedom *from* the ego, not freedom *for* the ego. The final understanding is not the result of seeking, but brings freedom from seeking. It is not about fulfilling expectations, but about being free of them. There are no future rewards in store. This very clarity turns out to be its own reward. Like Zen Master Hakuin exclaimed:

> *This very land is the pure lotus land,*
> *This very body is the body of Buddha!*

Nothing changes, but everything is released from its conceptual mold, as well as from the person who tried to fit life into the mold. Life's freshness is recognized; its presence is acknowledged; its oneness is seen – but by no one. There simply is recognition, acknowledgment, and seeing.

All this text will do is remind you of your true identity. It is not about self-improvement or methods. It contains no seven-step-systems to help you become more relaxed, more loving, or more fulfilled. If that is what you're looking for, there are plenty of other books and people that will cater to your needs.

If you want the truth, you have to look beyond the concepts of ego and self-improvement, and beyond the states of mind you would like to acquire. This book will explore – and attempt to puncture – the belief that you are a separate entity. It wants to point at the sourceless source from which all arises, and it asks you to remember that you are this source. Once this is recognized and it is clear what you truly are, you'll see that everything is exactly as it should be. It will not all fall magically into place. It already *is* and always has been in place.

This is not about a gradual progression to a future goal, but about a radical awakening to what is. No conditions have to be fulfilled for this to become clear. Self-realization can happen at any time for anyone. There can be quirky, irreverent, irritable characters who are certain about what they truly are and there can be relaxed, friendly, happy people who never even thought about so-called enlightenment. Calmness, friendliness, and happiness may or may not be or become part of your daily experience as a consequence of awakening, but at the same time it will become evident that this clarity is not about being in a good mood all the time. You don't need to do anything to 'become ready' for it. It will happen by itself and reveal that Awakeness is – and always has been – fully present. It will shine when it shines, and it will shift the attention from the content of Awareness to Pure Awareness itself. This Pure Awareness is what you truly are. When you think you're not it, this thought is part of the temporal content of Awareness and has no bearing on Awareness itself. Just let yourself be. Give yourself permission to be up, down, pissed or delirious. Observe the process and don't get caught in the content. Know yourself as the limitless field of Pure Awareness in which the drama of life merely arises.

For me this understanding has marked the end of my search and released me from the burden of trying to control my life and constantly improve myself. It did not set me free, but showed that I am freedom itself. It did not give me anything, but took 'the me' away. What I truly am is what I always was: Pure Awareness. This is true for you, the cat, the book, and everything else. To the mind, there seem to be separate objects; but in reality, everything emanates from the same essence. Seeing or not seeing this does not change anything. Everything simply is as it is, which is a lot less and infinitely more than I anticipated it to be.

2
Who is the author?

There has been gentle but persistent persuasion from people around me to include some of my personal history in this book. I felt some reluctance to do this, since confirming a personal story is – as will become clear later on – contradictory to what this book asserts. Furthermore, I had already included a description of 'my awakening' in the chapter *Blinded by the light*. My lady, however, pointed out that it is used there to illustrate what is being said in that chapter, rather than as an introduction to the me I once believed myself to be. As is so often the case, she was right.

From where I'm sitting, I can trace back several lines in space and time and arrive at a number of different 'histories' for this apparent individual. All are equally true and untrue; all are subjective and incomplete. Now that I've started, I will attempt to give you some background information and try to keep it relevant to my role as the author of this text, although any claim on my part to actually being the author contradicts what this book is about. Please keep this paradox in mind when you read the following linear description of the non-linear events experienced by this human being.

First, however, I'd like to share something from the Irish

scholar and philosopher who published his work under the pseudonym of Wei Wu Wei (1895 – 1986), although he certainly would never have claimed that it was 'he' who wrote it.

> *Tom, Dick, and Harry think they have written the books that they sign (or painted the pictures, composed the music, built the churches). But they exaggerate. It was a pen that did it, or some other implement. They held the pen? Yes, but the hand that held the pen was an implement too, and the brain that controlled the hand. They were intermediaries, instruments, just apparatus. Even the best apparatus does not need a personal name like Tom, Dick, or Harry.*
>
> *If the nameless builders of the Taj Mahal, of Chartres, of Rheims, of a hundred cathedral symphonies, knew that – and avoided the solecism of attributing to their own egos the works that were created through their instrumentality – may not even a jotter-down of passing metaphysical notions know it also?**

As for me, I was born in October of 1948 to a poor couple in Amsterdam. From an early age, I was familiarized with the idea that life has a spiritual dimension, although currently I no longer make the distinction between spiritual and non-spiritual. Psychic healers and clairvoyants were part of the crowd my parents hung out with. There were hand-laying sessions, divinations, and séances trying to contact 'the other world.'

Some of my earliest memories of 'spiritual' experiences

---

* From *Fingers pointing Towards The Moon: Reflections of a Pilgrim on the Way* by Wei Wu Wei. Sentient Publications

go back to a time when I was young enough to be put to bed when it was still light outside. The curtains would close, and a pattern of silver roses printed on a brick-colored background would allow a filtered light into the bedroom, creating the illusion of dancing creatures on the wall. At certain times I would lie awake and think about how there was nothing between the ceiling and me. I then tried to imagine what it would be like if there were no ceiling so that I could look into uninterrupted nothingness. I soon noticed that this little game would put me in a special state. A sensation, at once strange and pleasant, would come over me as my mind surrendered more deeply into the impossibility of imagining 'nothing.' When we would go to the park on a clear day, I would try to get at this 'nothing' by lying on my back and staring into the sky. Always, though, something – a bird, a cloud, or some grass – would enter my field of vision. Closing my eyes didn't work either, as swirling patterns seemed to dance on my retina and, at some point, I'd have to give up on the game.

When I was eight years old my parents divorced, and my two younger brothers and I stayed with my mother. In those days in Holland it still was not considered proper for a woman to be without a husband. Some people tried to help, but many others – neighbors, schoolteachers, and civil servants from the Social Security Office – made us feel judged. Bringing up three young boys was hard on my mother. She did the best she could, while my father was reluctant to chip in.

At one point, we converted to Catholicism. This was as much for the comfort of religion as for getting help from the church. It was my first brush with organized religion, and I took a very critical look at it. I hated going to church, but was intrigued by the religious teachings we received at my new Catholic school. There seemed to be an endless supply of fascinating stories from the Bible, but I soon noticed that my probing questions were not always appreciated. Whom did the children of Adam and Eve marry? If God is good, why is there so much injustice? How could a God of love destroy whole cities just because most of the people in them did not live by his commandments; and why did he send people to Hell to burn for eternity? Sometimes they told me that certain Bible stories where symbolic; then at other times, they'd insist that the Bible had to be taken literally.

Another mystery was that eating fish on Friday was considered to be fasting, while it was obviously feasting. The Friday lunch – served with white wine – was the highlight of the week for the priests of our parish.

We learned that all people were equal in the sight of God, but the richer people would have reserved places with softer kneeling cushions in the front rows of the church. It all seemed confusing, and it was clear that there were more questions than answers. I suppose that being introduced to the faith at a later age than the other kids at school made it more difficult for me to just accept what I was told. This made me a seeker, distrustful of spiritual authority.

Even then, I believed that there must be more to life than meets the eye. I believed in God, but could not accept what I was taught about him. By the age of twelve, I came upon an advertisement for a correspondence course in Raja Yoga. I persuaded my mother to sign up for it, and we started to receive regular lessons in the mail. The teacher was a professor of oriental studies. Although much in his texts was beyond my comprehension, something kept me going. There were new words and ideas about God, the Self, and life as a whole that sounded more real than that which I was hearing about at school.

As I got a little older, it became time to choose between continuing school and taking a job. Neither option seemed appealing. I wanted to draw or paint or have an adventurous life of travel and exploration. It was the sixties, and I learned to smoke hashish. I was still a minor, and the authorities that kept an eye on the children of divorced parents decided that I would be better off in a state home for difficult children. I'm sure they meant well, but at the time I did not see it that way.

In this place I mixed with kids who were there for more serious matters, such as car theft, burglary, and rape. I was told that I was there as a preventive measure, while most of the others where there as a punishment. I failed to see the fairness in this and escaped with one of the 'punished kids' who, even at this early age, was a skilled survivor. He knew how to open a safe, and I was an apt pupil.

I was now living on the streets. I hitchhiked throughout Europe and learned about hard drugs and needles. Finally psychedelics – especially LSD – took me away from addiction and brought me back to a more balanced state.

I became a macrobiotic hippy, got married, and had my first daughter, Leela. I was back reading and meditating and indulging my interest in all things mystical. Like many others of my generation, I made an overland trip to India. Along the road were new cultures, time to read, to party, and to practice yoga; though, I must say, spiritual practices did not really do it for me. There was no specific teacher. Alan Watts' books were my guiding light and main inspiration; but life was the real teacher and, somehow, whatever was appropriate to my search's unfolding presented itself, although I often did not recognize it at the time.

Looking back I can see how in magic moments I occasionally glimpsed this living presence appearing openly as, and at the same time hidden in, everything. It is for this reason that several people, including Wei Wu Wei and Tony Parsons, have referred to this as 'the open secret.'

During this journey there were so-called mystical or peak experiences; but in the end, all I can say is that there has been pain and pleasure, loss and gain, times of poverty and times of riches, parties and prisons, hospitals and health. There have been moments of despair on white sandy beaches and moments of great freedom in cold dank cells with iron bars.

In and through all this, the seeking continued, but in retrospect, nothing in the search can be assigned a function or meaning that, in itself, led to awakening – unless we consider giving up the search as a consequence of that search. The search consisted of acquiring information and experiences, while awakening was and continuously is revealed in the dropping of concepts and expectations. This dropping has happened by itself and not as an act of my personal will. In the process, this supposed individual's story was dropped as well, and even as I tell it, there is no one left to claim either the prize of enlightenment or the authorship of this text. Perhaps it is clear to you what this disclaimer means. If not, perhaps it will become clear during the reading of this book.

3

At the river's edge

You too are already on the other side. Enlightenment, or Self-realization, is not something that exists for only a select few. This book maintains that it is your true nature, right here and right now. Although it is a good idea to read it from the beginning, it is not, nor can it be, a linear how-to-get-enlightened manual. It is also not about self-improvement or the acquisition of knowledge. It is about the paradox of remembering what was never really forgotten. It's about who and what you truly are, not about what you should be or should become. You could think of it as a loom, weaving words into concepts that point at that which shines from beyond the realm of conceptual thinking.

All this book has to say in various ways is 'This is *it;* you are *it*,' and that's all there is to it. If reading it just once is enough for you, great; but if you're a seeker or simply in love with this subject, you can use the text to explore this message through such ideas and concepts as enlightenment, the ego, the intellect, the body, death, spiritual practices, the position of teachers, and your identity as a seeker. It talks about the surprise of *re*-cognizing the mystery of our collective and true identity and about *re*-membering the treasure trove within. It is not intended to make converts or to replace old beliefs and concepts with new ones. It is not about something I have or know, but you don't. It talks about Pure Awareness which, in the final analysis, is all there is. That being true, then ipso facto, whether acknowledged or unacknowledged, whether there is an apparent seeking for enlightenment or not, *you are IT*.

This text can serve as a small nudge, which if delivered at the right moment, can trigger an awakening in the same way that a snowball can trigger an avalanche. The following story of the master printing-press technician illustrates this point nicely:

A publishing company owned a huge printing press, which was essential to its business. One morning, after years of faithful service, the machine did not want to start. The company's technical people tried in vain to revive it. They finally gave up and contacted an expert who lived on the other side of the country. The next evening he arrived. It was too late to start work so he checked into a hotel for the night.

First thing in the morning, he took his tool kit over to the publisher and was shown the silent machine. He walked around it, did some tests, and found nothing wrong, except for the fact that vibrating over years of service had caused the press to be less than level, which prevented it from starting up. He did some measuring, took a wedge from his tool kit, and decided on the exact spot between the floor and the machine to insert it. He then gave it a few delicate taps with a hammer, flipped the switch, and the machine came instantly to life. The company was delighted with the quick result, but thought the bill of $2,700 excessive. When the master technician was asked to explain, he broke down his bill as follows:

$450 for the plane fare;
$150 for food and hotel;
$ 90 for his time;
$10 dollars for the wedge to level the machine;
and finally, $2,000 for knowing where and how to apply it.

This book can be such a wedge. Nothing needs to be repaired. You are whole as you are. The (re)activation of this understanding simply depends on whether or not it is the appropriate moment for you to 'level' with yourself. In the east, it is said that at such a moment of ripening the Guru will appear. This does not necessarily mean that one fine morning the doorbell will ring and a sage will be standing there saying, 'Good morning, dear seeker of the truth. It has been brought to my attention that you have reached the point where you're ready to receive THE ANSWER, and I am here to deliver it.'

What it does mean is that the invitation to see who you really are is always right here. What in eastern traditions is called the *guru* is that which extends the invitation. The guru (G-U-R-U) can appear as a person, but is not a person. Rather, the guru is a manifestation of the animating energy that appears in and as everything. It is life itself.

It is the inner consciousness by which he is unceasingly revealing his existence. This divine upadesa (instruction) is always going on naturally in everyone.*

Sri Ramana Maharshi

As long as we look through the distorted glass of our personal needs and opinions, we overlook this ever-present invitation. The data we select from the totality of our experience is filtered primarily for its relevance to our survival and immediate needs and desires. We look, amongst other things, for nourishment, sexual partners, social status, and security. This divides our sensory input into two basic categories: usable and unusable data. The usable data are admitted to *head*quarters, while the vast majority of signals get ignored. This way of managing information may be an extremely effective survival strategy, but it comes at the price of limited sensitivity and perception.

Next to fulfilling our concrete and basic material needs, we also use this data-management system to sustain our more abstract ego needs by looking for confirmation of our opinions and beliefs. We sift through the constant stream of information for whatever serves our needs or confirms what we accept as true. This selective perception operates on all levels from the obvious to the less obvious. For

---

* From *The Power of the Presence* by David Godman

example: You just bought a VW Beetle, and all of a sudden you notice Volkswagens everywhere. If you are in love with someone, you might be blinded to their shortcomings; while if you are prejudiced against a certain racial group, you will tend to overlook or discount the positive actions and characteristics of members of that group in favor of that which supports your opinion. Of course the VW Beetles were always there; your beloved is just as perfect or flawed as anyone else; and all races contain some people who are kind, some who are cruel, some who are wise, and some who are foolish. What you see is determined to a great extent by your 'inner selection committee,' much like it is for the travelers in the following Sufi story:

> *Upon entering a new country a traveler noticed an old man sitting under a tree. He approached him and asked about the people in his land. The old man answered by asking, 'How are the people in your country?'*
>
> *'Oh' said the traveler, 'they are friendly, hospitable, and cheerful.' 'Well,' the old man said, 'you'll find them to be the same in my country.'*
>
> *A few days later another traveler came up to the man under the tree with the same question, and again the old man responded by asking how the people in the traveler's country were.*
>
> *'They are always in a rush, they have very little time for each other, and their main concern in life is how much money they can make.'*
>
> *The old man shrugged and said, 'You'll find them to be the same in my country.'*

When, at some point, there is a spontaneous surrender

of the personal needs, preferences, desires, opinions, and beliefs that function as 'reality filters,' the realization of your true identity may spontaneously arise. When this happens there will be no more questions. You see that everything is the answer – that the guru is and has always been completely present. He manifests as the person, inner voice, or happening that triggers this surrender. Any way the invitation is extended, it functions as the guru. It may be silence from a sage or words from a shopkeeper. The surrender may come through agony or ecstasy. It can happen through an apple falling on your head; it can come from the smile of a child; or it can arise from deep inside as you walk along a beach at sunset or when you burn your finger on the stove. At any time, your sense of separation may dissolve to reveal the One beyond all duality. As a Zen master wrote on awakening to his true nature:

When I heard the temple bell ring,
suddenly there was no bell and no I,
just sound. *

Finally, yet importantly, there are no answers here, except those you are ready to give yourself. If this book resonates with you in such a way that it leads to insight, it will be by grace and not through the writer's or reader's accomplishment. In fact, as said in the previous chapter, this text will attempt to show that there is neither reader nor author. These words are nothing but a gentle reminder from yourself to yourself that you are the awakened one.

---

* From *Nonduality: A Study in Comparative Philosophy* by David Loy. Humanity Books

4

All you read here is NOT the truth!

The Tao Te Ching starts by affirming that: *'The Tao that can be spoken is not the true Tao.'* At this point, we might expect Lao Tsu to shut up and throw his brush and rice paper to the wind. Instead, he continues to expound for eighty-one chapters on the Tao of which one cannot speak.

In my country, there is a proverb that may explain this. It says, 'The mouth has no choice but to speak of *that* which fills the heart.' Compare it to a man in love who cannot stop talking about his lady. His intention is not to convince his friends to go and court her; he simply is unable *not* to talk about her. He may even write her long love letters in which he says he can't find the words to express the love in his heart. When the lady in question shares his feelings, she understands what is meant, regardless of his admitted inability to accurately tell her his feelings.

In a similar way, this text is also about what cannot be captured in words; but that is not to say you won't get its message. It is not a message that is meant to convert you, but is simply that which fills my heart – and like most men in love, I love to share it. It would, however, be nearer the truth to say that it is *that* which shares *itself* – *That* being what we all have in common, the luminous, self-aware center of our collective being.

Now we come to the disclaimer: You are advised to read carefully before swallowing any of the concepts contained in this book. They do not contain the truth, in the same way that the concept of water will not quench your thirst. Furthermore, they may be hazardous to your ego, your convictions, and your current values. Caution is advised in cases of extreme rigidity, since reading this book may lead to uncomfortable bending, stretching, or even to the annihilation of one's model of reality. Of course, you have to take even this disclaimer with a pinch of salt, as it is one of the concepts it warns you about.

Throughout this text, I'll keep reminding you of the book's conceptual nature and of the fact that this writing is simply a pointer or signpost, constantly repeating the same directions in different ways. Climbing the signpost will not get you to your destination. It is like Zen describing itself as 'a finger pointing to the moon.' If you focus on the finger, you will miss the luminosity at which it is pointing.

The moon for this textual finger is the ultimate subject, or *that which cannot be made into an object*. It is the source beyond space and time, which escapes all attempts at labeling and yet has been given many names, such as God, the ultimate ground of being, The Tao, your original face, or the deep Self (which, as you may have noticed, I distinguish by using the upper case S: Self).

This source is what you truly are; it is your true nature, your true home, your birthright, and a treasure you have apparently forgotten. Once this treasure is re-cognized or *dis*-covered, you know your true self (your Self) to be immortal and unborn, eternal and beyond time and space. You will be like the poor man in the children's story who suddenly finds out that his father is, in fact, the king. This re-membering is called Self-realization or enlightenment, clarity, or the final understanding. It doesn't matter what you call it. Pick whatever label you feel comfortable with. They all point to the same truth of what you really are.

Although I do not promote a specific religious, scientific, or philosophical system, I will freely quote from various sources. These quotes may be colored by the cultural or social context from which they come, but I find it utterly fascinating that voices from such different backgrounds as western and oriental philosophy, religion, and science – often centuries apart – speak of the same intimate essence.

In order to get the most from your reading, just be open and feel if this writing touches something real within you. See if it turns your inner compass to the true north of what you actually are.

The final and insurmountable problem with words is that, like the compass, they can point *from*, but never *at* the center from which the pointing is done. To those who will look both to where and from where the compass points, the realization of their true nature is directly available. In this knowing, the knower and the known are realized as inseparable and dissolve into the undivided space of Pure Awareness.

5

Do not be intimidated

In the previous chapters, some rather intimidating words were used – words like God, ultimate, immortal, and beyond space/time. Although these words are still insufficient to describe the indescribable, they also tend to hide the pure simplicity inherent in Self-realization. Enlightenment is not something difficult and remote, attainable only by an elite few. In fact, it is not *attainable* at all, but reveals itself through the removal of the illusion that there *is* an individual entity to take hold of it. It is fully present as Pure Awareness, not waiting to be realized somewhere else or in the future. It is not an event in space-time. On the contrary, space-time is an event in Pure Awareness, which is constantly manifesting itself as you, me, and all there is. It is these words, the reading of these words, and the background on which they appear; it is your breath going in and out, the beating of your heart, the smell of fresh coffee in the morning, the dog doo on the sidewalk, the stars, the planets, and the boundless space in which all this occurs. It is all of this, and at the same time, it is beyond all this. It is the container and perceiver, the creator and destroyer of all. It is as it is, including the idea that there is understanding here and the idea of a 'me' not understanding it. As a Zen text states:

If you understand, things are just as they are.
If you do not understand, things are just as they are.

If this is clear, just throw away the book, use it for kindling, or give it to a friend. If not, let us see if there is a way to progress to understanding or, perhaps surprisingly, to the realization that the very belief in a progressive path may be an obstacle to understanding. Could it be that we are walking around in search of the light while carrying a lit lantern?

6

Saints, sinners, seekers and sages

There is only one Guru, ever present,
The whole universe is His ashram,
No need for a path that leads to here,
No need to meditate for all is sacred,
No need to find what never was lost.

If you have come this far in the text and are still reading, chances are good that you are what is known as a seeker. Many seekers sincerely believe that they want to find the truth and that this truth will set them free. The fact of the matter is that, more often than not, they have already decided on what this truth should be like. For starters, there frequently is the belief that this truth is something objective and obtainable. Next comes the assumption that there is a path leading to truth, freedom, enlightenment, or Self-realization, and that this path can be shown to the seeker by an enlightened master. 'Getting it' – or so one hopes – is achieved by following this path.

In the spiritual marketplace we find an abundance of paths from which to choose, and the seeker usually shops around for one that suits him. Meister Eckhart, a German Christian mystic who lived from 1260 until 1328, says this about such a path:

For whoever seeks God in some special way, will gain the way and lose God who is hidden in the way. But whoever seeks God without any special way, finds Him as He really is... and He is life itself.

Most of these paths are concerned with restrictions, discipline and, in one way or another, being good. How restrictions and discipline can lead to freedom is not entirely clear, but all the same, the seeker believes that by diligently following the chosen path, his efforts will give him merit. This should qualify him for a cosmic promotion. God, or whatever name one has for the ultimate, is expected to reward these efforts; either through revealing him/herself or by bestowing his/her grace upon the seeker in the form of a grand and final 'happening' that reveals the truth. This revelation supposedly is, or will result in the attainment of, enlightenment. Enlightenment, in this scenario, is seen as a most desirable state. It should, once and for all, get rid of life's problems and transform the seeker's personality, resulting in pure thoughts, right action, radiant love, and a condition of eternal bliss.

Usually the seeker looks for a master or sage who can help deliver the experience. This 'enlightened one' should not only be a sage, but is typically expected to be a saint, as well. The various 'guru wish lists' held by seekers reflect this idea and feature all kinds of desirable character traits such as loving, forgiving, patient, ascetic, vegetarian, charismatic, etc. Preferably, the sage is silver haired, comes from the east, dresses in exotic garments, and has a presence that transmits a magical vibration.

To those seekers who have not closed this book in

disgust, I admit that for effect's sake, the above-sketched picture is one-dimensional. The sincere seeker appears to invest his pursuit with lots of feeling, energy, and dedication. I say 'appears to invest,' because the moment of 'finding' will show that there never really was a seeker; that what appeared as the seeker was that which was being sought. It is like a game of hide and seek played by one. The seeker and the finder, the teacher and the student are all guises of the one Self.

On meeting one's true teacher, it is indeed possible to be emotionally overwhelmed; but in truth, it is Self-meeting-Self. If or when such a connection happens, the magic that comes through is as much in the seeker as in the sage. It is like two flames recognizing that they are one-and-the-same fire. The manifestation of this energy as the teacher/student interaction, is something that – like falling in love – happens spontaneously, not something that is done by going after some fixed ideas one holds to be true.

This is not to say you have to wait for such a happening. The real teacher is life itself. The invitation to see this is extended in this very moment, and the guidance of a formal teacher, while helpful to many, is not needed. There are no fixed rules as to how awakening should occur. The problem with preconceived notions about the much-coveted holy grail of truth and the packaging in which it should be delivered, is that such notions prevent the seeker from seeing that the liberation he is looking for is always fully present and instantly available. Ramana Maharshi said:

Make no effort to work or to renounce; your very effort is bondage.

Instead of directly seeing *what is*, the seeker continues to wait for a future event of enlightenment, not admitting that he's already – and always has been – home. He often tries to anticipate what it would be like to reach a final and total understanding in which God and the universe reveal their secrets. In doing so he overlooks the fact that his mind is both part of and appearing *in* this universe and, thus, is not qualified to comprehend it.

As the following quotes show, even the best among us get caught up in assumptions about the absolute:

> **Einstein:** *'God does not play dice.'*
> **Einstein:** *'God is not malicious.'*
> **Bohr:**[*] *'Einstein, stop telling God what to do!'*

Giving up one's expectations in favor of a willingness to simply accept *what is* may create a vacuum that could be filled with surprising alternatives. For instance, it might be recognized that finding does not come from seeking, but that it may be revealed through giving up the search; that it is not something to see, but the seeing itself; that cherished beliefs might be unmasked as conceptual obstacles, and spiritual practices may turn out to be a way of avoiding a direct seeing into the heart of the matter. This direct seeing exposes the illusion of a separate seeker who can arrive at 'destination enlightenment' somewhere in the future. Consequently, the seeking and the seeker are both annihilated in the realization that he *is* already home.

To the exhausted seeker I would like to say, 'Drop the search and drop your concepts. Stop looking for your ass. Just sit down and relax.' Letting go of your preconceived

---

[*] Niels Bohr (1885 1962): Danish physicist

notions could suddenly shift your attention from the far-off horizon at which you gaze in anticipation of a grand and extraordinary event and reveal the wonder that exists right in front of, behind, and in your own eyes. Through this letting go, you may find yourself open to – and possibly even in the presence of – the most unlikely of masters.

Let it be clear, however, that Pure Awareness is all there is, and any concept of a master 'out there' only exists from the perspective of an imaginary seeker. True masters, therefore, do not consider themselves masters at all, but know that you consider yourself a disciple. They will tell you that you are it; and when you say 'Yes but,' they will repeat the same truth or tell you to relax or to sweep the floor or to keep silent; or, perhaps, they will keep silent themselves. Whatever they say, do, or don't do, they are probably not as you had pictured them.

Can you imagine a sage owning a tobacco store, being a smoker, and living in a big city on the fringe of the red-light district? Well, there was such a teacher. This shopkeeper, who apparently also had quite a temper, took care of his children and received seekers from all over the world. He communicated with them through interpreters/ translators, although he seemed to have been able to speak English. The reader may have already recognized Sri Nisargadatta Maharaj, one of the most respected sages of the 20th century.

Here is a dialogue between a seeker and Sri Nisargadatta Maharaj:

Seeker: *I was told that a realized person will never do anything unseemly. That they will behave in an exemplary way.*

Sri Nisargadatta Maharaj: *Who sets the example? Why should a liberated one necessarily follow conventions? The moment one becomes predictable, one cannot be free.**

Or how about his pupil Ramesh Balsekar? He's a patient family man who welcomes seekers from all over the planet, not in an ashram, but in his Mumbai home. Ramesh is a retired bank manager and an awakened teacher/author on the subject of Nonduality/Advaita. This is what he once said about his teaching:

If you have heard something here, fine. If not, fine. If some change is to occur as a consequence, let it take place. If the understanding at any level has any value, any worth, it must naturally work its own way out. No 'one' can do it. **

Another teacher I would like to mention is Tony Parsons from the UK. He is an accessible, (extra)ordinary, and friendly person, who is more into sharing (t)his presence than in teaching from the top down. Even as I write this, I can hear him say, 'There is no one here to share. There is only presence; This is it; This is The Beloved.' He strips away all belief that there is a future event of enlightenment one should go after and invites the seeker to see *what is*. In his book *As It Is* he says:

This is it, and that's the end of it. Give up the search for something to happen and fall in love, fall intimately in love with the gift of presence in What Is. Here, right here, is the seat of all that you will ever long for. It is simple

---

* From *I Am That*. Chetana Publications, Mumbai, India.
** From *Sin And Guilt*. Zen Publications, Mumbai, India.

*and ordinary and magnificent. You see, you are already home.**

The last sage I want to introduce here, and one who definitely does not fit the holy-man mold, is Wayne Liquorman, an American publisher/author and disciple of Ramesh Balsekar. He never makes a secret of his former life as an alcoholic. He even refers to this period by calling himself a pig who just wanted more – more booze, more drugs, more sex – more, more. And more was simply not enough. One day he woke up and was struck sober. In his own words:

*Then there came at the end of a four-day binge a moment of absolute certainty that that phase of my life was over. It was like a switch had been thrown. The obsession was gone. It wasn't a matter of having to resist or do anything. It was gone. And what was staggeringly clear is that I hadn't done it. If I hadn't done it, the question then became, 'What has done this to me? If I am not the master of my destiny, what is?' This was the point at which my head went into the tiger's mouth, the jaws closed, and there was no escape. I became a seeker. ***

If you meet Wayne now, you meet a big man with a big laugh and a big sense of humor. In his book *Acceptance of What Is* he says about seekers that come to see him:

'Lots of people come here, and if what I say agrees with what they already know and believe is true, then they

* From *As It Is*. Inner Directions Publishing.
** From: http://www.advaita.org/ Wayne Liquorman interviewed by Blayne Bardo, May 1998.

say, 'This guy really knows what he's talking about. He's okay!' (laughter) And if what I'm saying does not agree with what they already know or believe to be the truth, they say, 'He's full of shit,' and they go on down the road.' *

Unconventional sages are not just from our time. As a poem attributed to Shankara, the 8th century Indian philosopher and father of Advaita Vedanta, puts it:

Sometimes, naked, sometimes mad,
Now as scholars, now as fools,
Thus they appear on the earth –
The free men!

When we read about the Zen masters and Taoist sages of old times, we might encounter some pretty rough fellows, some of them wielding sticks, slapping students, getting drunk, or even removing a wooden statue of Buddha from a temple to make a fire on a cold night. All this is not to suggest that rascally sages are the only true sages, as this would again be an attempt to create an image to which the preferred sage should conform. Nor is it meant to suggest that a sage could never be a saint, but only that a sage needn't be – that a sage may as well be a housewife, a soldier, or a businessman. If expectations about the truth being sought and the sages who 'know' are dropped, one may find unexpected treasure right in one's own back yard. Accepting that sages are simply human and not super human makes it easier for you to accept yourself just the way you are. It relaxes unrealistic expectations about

---

* From *Acceptance of What Is, A Book About Nothing.* Advaita Press

teachers and about what you think you should become. Your truth and freedom lie in the way you are right now, in accepting *what is*.

Rumi said:

Do not look at my outward shape, but take what is in my hand.

So, what is being offered here? What exactly is in this hand? Is it something we can perceive, receive, and take hold of, or at the very least, is it something we can comprehend?

7
Do you get it?

Science cannot solve the ultimate mystery in nature. And it is because in the last analysis we ourselves are part of the mystery we try to solve.[*]

It is often said that enlightenment is beyond the intellect's grasp. This chapter will investigate that claim, which raises much suspicion in the mind. Nebulous references, such as *All is One*; *This is it;* and *Beyond space and time* do not hack it. The intellect insists on facts and is sure that if someone would just explain enlightenment properly, it would definitely get it. The following story illustrates that hearing the right answer is not always as helpful as we might expect.

In his book, The Hitchhikers Guide to the Galaxy, *Douglas Adams tells us of an earthling, Arthur Dent, who escapes our planet just moments before it is demolished to make room for an intergalactic highway. The Hitchhikers Guide becomes his indispensable travel companion and the guide's motto 'don't panic' sees him through many adventures.*

---

[*] Max Planck (Karl Ernst Ludwig) (1858-1947) Theoretical physicist

While traveling between the stars, Arthur Dent hears the story of a super computer named 'Deep Thought,' built by an alien race to answer the ultimate question of 'Life, The Universe, and Everything.' After seven-and-a-half million years of calculating, Deep Thought comes back with the result. Dignitaries, priests, and scientists gather to learn the answer. And the answer is (drum roll, please).........42!

Well, 42 might be the correct answer, but without a first-hand understanding as to how Deep Thought arrived at it, this answer is useless. The same is true for the answer to the question 'What is enlightenment?' Those who 'know' insist that it is beyond the intellectual mind and, at the same time, that it is simplicity itself. One may tell you that there is no enlightenment and no one to become enlightened, while another will say that enlightenment is already fully present. Although they seem to contradict each other, they are both pointing back to the same indefinable center from which the pointing is done. They might tell you that if this is not clear, no answer will satisfy you, and any answer you might be given will only be understood as an invitation to ask the next question.

The intellect, however, is convinced that to each question there is a comprehensible and 'right' answer. It says: 'Just be clear with me and don't tell me that this understanding is beyond me. Did I not build the pyramids, bring forth the theory of relativity, put a man on the moon, and map the human genome?'

Yes indeed, the intellect apparently did all these things and much, much more; but please note the use of the word *apparently* here. It's important because, when there is clarity as to what enlightenment is or what it is not, one's perspective on the activating energy in all thinking and doing shifts from the personal to the impersonal.

When, in the current intellectual climate, we talk about the mind, we generally mean the intellect. This has not always been the case. In Zen texts, for example, we regularly encounter the term *Buddha-Mind*, which stands for what in this text is called Pure Awareness. The word mind is also often used as the polar opposite of the word heart, defining the intellect as opposed to the center of emotion. More recently, we have started to divide the intellect and emotions between the brain's left and right hemispheres, where – to put it very simply – the left hemisphere is the seat of our linguistic ability and the intellect, while the right hemisphere is the intuitive and emotional partner. Humanity, with its analytical approach to life, has increasingly put its faith in the left hemisphere. The left hemisphere is wary of the right hemisphere's 'fuzzy logic' and jealously guards its dominant position, all with the best intentions, as it sincerely believes it's the 'best man for the job.'

'Man' is the right word here, since masculinity is more representative of the left hemisphere's methodology. This dominance is reflected in society at large where, in many situations, women are still not seen as equal to men and where many corporate and political undertakings are devoid of the balancing influence of the heart. We only have to open our eyes to see what a folly this one-sided approach to life actually is.

The intuitive mind is a sacred gift and the rational mind is a faithful servant.

We have created a society that honors the servant and has forgotten the gift.

Albert Einstein

The left side may, indeed, be the better suited for dividing and categorizing the world into dualistic terms; but what is discussed here points to the non-dual – to Pure Awareness – as the totality in and from which the mind and its activity arises.

The rational mind excels in making appointments, balancing the books, organizing parties, making bombs, designing buildings, and a million other tasks; but it is totally out of its league when it comes to non-duality and unconditioned, concept-free Pure Awareness. It's simply impossible to grasp what 'free from concepts' means, because until there is understanding, it is just another concept. It's equally impossible to understand the non-dual perspective from the dualistic position of *someone who understands* on the one hand, and *that which is understood* on the other.

Understanding, however, *is* possible from the position of the single activity that remains when the apparent separation between subject and object has been dissolved. That there could be understanding without this traditional dualistic relationship is an unfamiliar idea, but perhaps it can be glimpsed when compared to the relationship between a thought and the thinker of this thought. This division is merely a grammatical convention because there has never been a thought independent of a thinker. In reality, thought and thinker constitute a single process of thinking. In a similar sense, the one who understands and that which is understood can be seen as a single process of understanding. The instant that the one who understands and that which is understood merge, there is no one left to get it, and only understanding remains.

Studying the Taste of Apples

In relation to Pure Awareness, the best the intellect can do is to recognize its own *modus operandi*. In other words, to get it, we must get *why* we cannot get it. If, at this point, the intellectual mind does not see its natural limitations, it may jump to a wrong conclusion like, 'Oh if I can't get it, it must be complicated.' No doubt about it, trying to capture the non-dual in the dualistic medium of language can get very complicated; but in essence, it is not complicated at all, just as pointing out the color blue to a child is simple, but explaining it to a professor who was born blind is next to impossible.

While the heart – or right hemisphere of the brain – has a feel for this type of reasoning, the dividing and classifying left-brained aspect doesn't. It is simply not the correct tool for dealing with the undivided whole to which this text is pointing. The intellect is the wrong tool for relating to non-dualistic reality, in the same way that a bucket is the wrong tool for scooping up the summer wind, or that bars are unfit to confine the rain, or that a sealed coffin can't hold sunlight.

The mind not only appears *in* Awareness, it tends to confuse its own intellectual activity *with* Awareness. In fact, Awareness is not a product of the mind, but the mind is a product of Awareness – the silent and permanent background common to everything, *including* the mind and its activity. Like the screen on which we watch a movie, this background is generally ignored in favor of the impermanent activity that appears on or against it. Zoom out, and Awareness and its content unify in a Self-luminous singularity about which nothing can be said or known for the simple reason that anything said or known is part-and-parcel of this singularity.

*May not thought itself thus be a part of reality as a whole? But then, what could it mean for one part of reality to 'know' another, and to what extent would this be possible?**

This says that an observer can never take up a position outside of totality to observe and evaluate that totality. In

* *Wholeness and the Implicate Order* by David Bohm. Routledge & Kegan Paul

other words, there cannot be a *you* separate from totality that can intellectually get at totality. Pure Awareness in and from which all arises is your true identity. Similar to the light, which is unable to shine on itself, you cannot *get* it, because you *are it*.

You may realize this or you may think, 'Great, but what good does it do me that I *am it* even when I don't get it?' If this is the case, let's try another approach. Let's just forget about getting it or not getting it and, instead, investigate this 'I' or 'me' that does not get it.

8

The notion of 'me'

For many, the greatest obstacle to seeing that there already is enlightenment is the illusion that they exist as a separate individual with a so called ego. When one feels himself to be such a separate entity, yet accepts the suggestion that the ego is false, he may feel the need to get rid of this illusion. He often believes that he has to go through a lengthy process of discipline, purification, and practice, which may perhaps even take several lifetimes, before he will be able to break free and become enlightened.

Stating that being a separate individual is an illusion may sound like a bold claim, but neither contemporary western science nor eastern mystical traditions confirm the existence of a separate self. Objectively, there is no proof for this 'me.' Subjectively, however, most of us are convinced of its reality. The next three chapters are dedicated to dissecting this belief. We will approach this apparent certainty from different angles and see how much substance there is to the idea. Nothing said here is meant to tell you to get rid of your ego, but rather it endeavors to show you that there really is no independent ego, just like there are no waves independent of the ocean.

We are accustomed to thinking of ourselves as autonomous centers of consciousness residing in bodies.

We identify with a self that is either the origin of our actions, thoughts, and feelings or is a subject to which stuff happens. This experience of being a separate entity with likes and dislikes, possessions, opinions, relations, and responsibilities is something almost all of us share. We think of this unique mix as our personality. While we know our personality as a dynamic flux that can be altered by experience, the ego is thought to be the permanent self, that which remains intact as life modifies the makeup of the personality: The 'I' that first was a child and now is an adult, or the 'I' that first did not like tomatoes and now loves them. This conviction of being a separate entity with a unique personality is reflected in our social conditioning, our values, and the structure of our language.

Our social conditioning and education are geared to make us into responsible individuals through emphasizing and confirming our uniqueness. We are encouraged to take credit for our achievements and to accept personal responsibility for our thoughts and deeds. Just how responsible we really are is an open question. A lot of the thoughts and opinions we claim as 'ours' are, in fact, more due to circumstances than to choice. In the Christian worldview, some of the most cherished values and beliefs center around individual responsibility and God's gift of free will. Someone born into another context, however, may know with equal certainty that there is no individual free will, but only God's will. A closer look at our ideas and opinions reveals that they come, to a large degree, from our programming, which in turn, depends mainly on which socio-cultural group we are born into, as well as on the attitude and status of our educators within that group. As we grow up, we generally accept the values, opinions, and beliefs gleaned from this conditioning as 'ours.' When a child is born in Palestine, it soon knows Israel to be in the wrong; while the child born in Israel knows exactly the opposite.

Further suppositions accepted as truth come from our use of language. If we listen closely to the way words are commonly used, they will reveal our underlying – and for the most part unexamined – assumptions. After a certain point, it becomes very difficult to know to what extent the use of words expresses the way we see the world and to what extent language actually shapes that world.

> *The twentieth-century linguistic revolution is the recognition that language is not merely a device for communicating ideas about the world, but rather a tool for bringing the world into existence in the first place. Reality is not simply 'experienced' or 'reflected' in language' but instead is actually produced by language.*[*]

From this perspective, words are powerful magic. When, for example, we teach our children the chant *'Sticks and stones may break my bones, but names can never hurt me,'* it's not truly reflecting a belief that words are without power; but it is, in fact, meant to be a counter-spell to ward off a verbal attack.

By dividing the world around us into named and labeled objects, we apparently gain the power to manipulate it to a certain degree; but through this practice we loose sight of the universal and primary oneness.

---

[*] Boston University anthropologist Misia Landau quoted in Roger Lewin's *In the Age of Mankind*. Smithsonian Institution

When we see two islands, are they separated by water, connected by water, or does the water hide their connection? Is there really a wave and an ocean, a fire and its flames, the water and its wetness, or, for that matter, a person and his environment?

In addition to these dualistic labels, our language is full of expressions that confirm identity and promote separation: *Be a man; She's a real person; It's us against them* and the less obvious *Conquering nature; Face up to reality*, and *Life is what you make it*. If we take these literally, as most of us do, we may conclude that we exist separately from nature and that nature – including our own human nature – has to be conquered; that reality is something we exist apart from and have to face up to; and that there is life on the one hand and us having to make something of it on the other.

As long as we realize that the symbols we use to describe our world are not that which they attempt to describe, there is no confusion. When we forget, however, that the map is not the territory, we get hypnotized into seeing the world as a complex and scrambled jigsaw puzzle, too big and complicated for us ever to completely put together. This way of thinking not only promotes the idea that we are separate from our environment, but it also encourages manipulation and exploitation *of,* instead of cooperation *with*, that environment.

The fact that we have a concept of 'our environment' hides the truth that the environment and we are, in reality, a single continuum; any biologist can tell you that the separate existence of a body-mind organism is an illusion. An organism appears in, and is inseparable from, its environment. This description still falls short of the unimaginable reality in which there is ultimately neither person nor environment. *Person* and *environment* are two labels slapped on, and thereby apparently dividing, a single event. Because it is a single phenomenon, there is no one to stand outside it to take hold of it. Walt Whitman expresses this sense of union with the environment as follows:

My tongue, every atom of my blood, formed from this soil, this air,
   *Born here of parents born here from parents the same, and their parents the same....**

Even when we agree with what the biologists or the poet Walt Whitman says, most of us do not feel this to be so. We experience ourselves as self-contained units, each with an individual existence, distinct from the world out there. This sense of being separate is one of the definitions of the word *ego*. We will get back to this later on in more detail, but for now it suffices to say that the words *ego* and *individual,* as used in this text, stand for the illusory sense of separation created at the point where Pure Awareness apparently forgets itself and identifies with a time-and-space-bound entity.

The dynamic processes of this entity appear as thoughts, feelings, experiences, and the body-mind organism. They are labeled as objective possessions: my thoughts, my feelings, my experiences, and my body.

Sadly, the body-mind is not a firm foundation for the ego to stand on. After some time, it falls apart and dies. Death is either seen as the end of 'me' (sort of like the captain going down with the ship) or there is a belief/hope that

---

* From *Song Of Myself* by Walt Whitman (1819 - 1892)

the 'me-essence' (a.k.a. the soul) will survive. Depending on one's belief, the soul either carries on without a body or will reincarnate into a new body.

Even though this 'me' may feel separate and lonely, it is clearly not alone. All around, there are countless 'me's' trying, with varying degrees of success, to run their own individual shows, each looking out for number one. From this perspective, the world appears as a collection of separate, impermanent objects and short-lived, mortal individuals – insignificant occurrences lost in the vastness of space and time. Even if our shared mortality inspires compassion in some, most of us feel alienated, not just from each other, but also from the environment and life as a whole. We may be doing fine in this instant, but just beneath the surface lurks the uneasy feeling that we are not truly at home in this vast and cold universe where, at any moment, something could go terribly wrong. Time seems to slip away from us at an alarming rate. The possibilities of disease, tragedy, and the infirmity in old age are always with us; and with a death sentence hanging over our head, there is a certain urgency to make the best of it before our time runs out. Such a perspective on life comes from the conviction that one is, indeed, a time-bound and mortal individual, an object amongst objects, existing in and having to deal with the bleak 'reality' I just sketched. This sense of separation is so deep-seated that it is rarely questioned. It seems to be an absolute and verifiable truth. I ask you, then, to verify it. Question this assumption, contemplate it, check it out, and discover if there really is any solid evidence for the existence of this 'me.'

9

The enemy within

Many teachings put forth the ego as the main obstacle to achieving the ultimate goal of true knowing. The seeker learns that the ego is an illusion and often buys into the idea that it is bad and the way to get enlightened is to kill it off.

The idea of this 'bad ego' gets associated with either our supposed animalistic nature, which needs to be disciplined, or with the religious belief that human nature is sinful and has to be conquered if one wants to go to Heaven. For several reasons, these are most curious concepts.

Before we can have a meaningful discussion of ego, it helps to recognize that the word means different things to different people. It is Latin for 'I,' and in psychoanalytic terms it stands for the core of the personality that deals with reality and, in turn, is influenced by it. In philosophy, the ego stands for the conscious self. There are many variations on these definitions, some of which overlap and some of which are incompatible. The ego is seen as:

- One's identity;
- One's consciousness of one's identity;
- An inflated feeling of pride or a sense of superiority towards others;

- One's personality or character;
- One's self-image;
- The thread of memory that gives us a sense of continuous presence;
- The combination of socio-cultural conditioning and genetic programming;
- An autonomous center of consciousness and volition inside a body;
- A dreamed-up character played by the true Self;
- A mistaken identity where the universal *I am* is taken to be a personal *I am so and so*.

In this text, we are mainly concerned with the philosophical concept of mistaken identity or the illusory ego. Since 'I' and ego are self-referent, 'me' attempting to get rid of 'my ego' is contradictory and consequently an impossible task. Below are a few examples that illustrate some of the inconsistencies that originate in the ego concept:

- While driving our car on a hot day we may encounter the optical illusion of water on an asphalt road without expecting to drive through it, but even when the seeker is convinced that the ego is an illusion, he continues to treat it as a reality. Somehow, we are able to simply discount the water-mirage on the road, but we continue to struggle with the mirage of the ego.

- Most seekers believe the ego to be an obstacle to enlightenment and try to get rid of it; but who is getting rid of whom, and what does one hope to accomplish? It usually comes down to: '*I* want to get rid of *my* ego, since *I* believe that this will get *me* (who?) what *I* desire. Of course, the ego is aware of all attempts on its life. It's like a convicted man who has been put in charge of his own execution. In an alleged conversation between Lao Tsu and Confucius, Lao Tsu says:

> *Your attempt to eliminate self is a positive manifestation of selfishness.*
>
> *You are like a person beating a drum in search of a fugitive.*

• The seeker, who wants to get rid of his ego chases an ever-receding illusion. First, he splits himself in two – the ego and the one trying to get rid of it. As he realizes this split, he then occupies a third position. As soon as he notices this third 'me' that sees both the ego and the one wanting to get rid of it, there must be a fourth 'me' seeing the third me, and then a fifth seeing the fourth, and so on. An endless subdivision starts, which reminds me of a limerick Alan Watts used to illustrate this point.

> *There was a young man who said:*
> *'Though it seems that I know that I know,*
> *What I would like to see, is the I that knows me,*
> *When I know, that I know, that I know.'*

• The whole undertaking of getting rid of the ego is a result of the desire to become enlightened, yet desire is supposedly one of the main obstacles that prevents enlightenment from occurring. Consequently, one seems to have no choice other than to desire not to desire, which, of course, is an impossible – and in essence egoic – assignment.

Considering the inherent contradictions in the 'get-rid-of-the-ego-concept,' eventually the seeker has to draw the conclusion that the whole effort of dropping the ego is doomed to failure. While this apparently depressing outcome seems to put liberation beyond one's reach, it is, in fact, a sign of hope because the idea that there is an 'I' (or ego) that can bring about its own liberation begins to disintegrate.

Wrestling with the ego's paradoxical nature will not, in itself, lead to insight; but it can clear the way for a spontaneous surrender through exhaustion. In this surrender, the ego problem does not so much get solved as dissolved. When the ego illusion breaks up, there is no one left to get enlightened, and what remains is the realization that enlightenment already is. By clearly understanding that this whole ego business is a juggling of incompatible ideas and self-contradictory concepts, it can vanish like a morning mist, revealing the rising sun.

From this insight one may come to the understanding that what was said from the beginning is true: The ego is an illusion. In fact, no one has ever seen or been able to produce a shred of solid evidence supporting the existence such an entity. Of course, not being able to prove something does not automatically disprove it. You cannot prove the content of a dream, but this does not mean that your account of it is untrue. The dream's content may not be provable, but science can show that dreaming does occur. For the ego's existence or absence, however, there is no such proof; there is only subjective confirmation. This personal 'evidence' has been studied over thousands of years. Those who say that the ego is an illusion first believed in its existence, but afterward they report that its absence is more real than its presence. What is left in the ego's absence is the clarity that your true being is Pure Awareness and that your sense of separation was a divine hypnosis making you experience yourself as a limited entity. Metaphorically, this experience of a separate self could be explained as nothing more than an expression of the true Self at play. In this metaphor, the ego is a limited character with no existence of its own. It is the true Self in one of its many guises, much like the villain in the movie, who does not exist apart from the actor pretending to be him.

Even when this reasoning is convincing on an intellectual level, the seeker may still be stuck with the undeniable sense that the ego does exist. This sense of ego-reality comes from the Self's mastery in weaving the illusion. It plays the characters so convincingly that they even include a sense of autonomy. Imagine you're reading a novel. On page twenty-five, the hero contemplates what to do. He seems to weigh his options and choose a course of action; but whatever he decides, the author has already written it out on page thirty. As the author of the book of life the Self ingeniously perpetuates the illusion of independence and volition, validating the ego even while fighting it with other illusions, such as spiritual practices. These attempts to beat the ego into submission actually continue the illusion of separation. In the words of Wei Wu Wei:

Destroy 'the ego,' hound it, beat it, snub it,

tell it where it gets off?
Great fun, no doubt, but where is it?
Must you not find it first?
Isn't there a word about catching your goose
before you can cook it?
… The great difficulty here is that there isn't one.*

The whole fight, 'the hounding, beating, and snubbing,' *IS* the ego illusion. The ego will fight as hard to survive as the seeker will fight to kill it. This appears to be a contradiction. How can one fight an illusion, and – even stranger – how can an illusion fight back? Well, it cannot. But true to its illusory nature, it *apparently* can, just as a dog can have the illusion that his tail is fleeing from him when he chases it. We could say that the ego illusion is not so much in perceiving the ego as it is in identifying with it. The ego has the same level of reality as an echo, which has no existence apart from the sound it reflects. It has as much substance as your shadow. No amount of effort will allow you to take hold of it, catch it under a blanket, or leave it behind.

We could compare this struggle with the ego to someone who tries to determine his weight by grabbing himself around the ankles and attempting to lift his body off the floor. The harder he pulls, the heavier he *seems*. This straining will create a feedback loop, confirming that there really is a weight too big for his strength. Apparent solutions are to start weight training to get stronger or to diet to become lighter. Either choice will continue the illusion that progress is being made and will re-enforce the belief that eventually the problem will be overcome.

---

* From *Posthumous Pieces* by We Wu Wei. Sentient Publications

Of course, it will not work since the whole problem *is* the attempt to overcome it. The perceived problem dissolves the instant one gives up the effort to resolve it. All of a sudden the person has his hands free for other things and can now easily move his own weight by simply walking, jumping, or dancing.

When the fight with the ego (sometimes masquerading as spiritual practice) is abandoned, the impersonal Self may reveal its true nature – the vital essence that is common to all that is. This vital essence plays hide and seek disguised as the body-mind organism of the seeker until it is ready to play 'find.'

When it is clear that all is one, the sense that there is a separate ego can only be an activity of the true Self. Why does it do this, you might ask? The most succinct answer is 'Why not?' The longer answer is that it does this because play is its very nature.

This play is what the Hindus call Leela, the cosmic dance of manifestation, or the activity in which the Self forgets that it is alone (or All-One). The Self loses itself in the dream of existence, which allows it to have the most terrifying and glorious adventures, just for the sake of the experience. From this point of view, there is no injustice in the world. When a murder takes place, the Self appears as the killer as well as the victim, the policeman who arrests the killer, and the judge who sends him to prison.

Compare this 'being lost in the game' to the way we forget ourselves when absorbed in a movie containing love scenes, betrayal, violence, and self-sacrifice. We may be outraged, shocked, or deeply touched and moved to tears; but at some level, we know we are safe at all times and that it is just a movie.

In the moment of surrender – the moment when the ego caves in – life is seen as the fabulous dream-game it is. At this instant, the search is over, and the hallucination of a separate self is exposed as a magical illusion produced by the universal Self. The personal identity dissolves into the Source just as a drop of spray reunites with the ocean.

If that happens, there will be no one left to read these words – although the words will not go unread. As long as 'you' are reading, however, let's have a look at that basic and undeniable sense of 'I am,' which should not be confused with the ego illusion.

10
I am ... or am I?

Did you ever attend a sand-sculpting contest on a beach? People make the most amazing copies of ancient statues or come up with their own designs, yet whatever they produce, it is still sand. When the statues collapse, they dissolve back into the beach. In much the same way, all appearances in Pure Awareness are nothing but Pure Awareness.

Out of Pure Awareness, out of this One Substance, arises the root thought of all thoughts: *I AM*. From this arises the ego through identification; appearing as 'I am so and so' and therefore 'I am not such and such.' An apparent division of what is essentially one unfolds, and all forms and beings come into existence.

The nameless is the beginning of heaven and earth.
*The named is the mother of ten thousand things.**

As the word *Uni*-verse implies, and as all the great religious traditions hold to be true, there is nothing (no-thing) outside of God. All Is One, and as such, the belief in a separate, mortal, and time-bound ego appearing in the

---

* From *Tao Te Ching* translated by Gia-Fu Feng and Jane English. Wildwood House Ltd.

multi-verse in which most of us apparently lead our lives, is an illusion.

When we introduce ourselves, we usually start with 'I am' followed by our name or profession. Upon investigation, however, it proves impossible to locate this 'I.' Although I certainly do have a name, I am not that name. The same goes for sensations, thoughts, and emotions. They cannot be who I am because their nature is impermanent and fleeting, while the sense of 'I' remains constant.

The 'I' that questions who it is can no more investigate itself than a mirror can reflect itself.

Here is a dialogue between Bodhidharma and Hui-k'o:

Hui-k'o: *My mind is not at peace. Please Master, pacify it for me.*
Bodhidharma: *Bring me your mind and I will pacify it for you.*
Hui-k'o: *When I look for it I cannot find it.*
Bodhidharma: *There, I have pacified your mind!*

Sensations, emotions, and thoughts simply arise without any evidence of a 'me' first deciding to have them. When I focus on the thought process – which seems more under my direct control than sensations and emotions – I cannot find the thinker who decides to have a certain thought before it occurs. Of course, I can say, 'Yes, it's me who decided to have this thought,' but this is just another thought. What's more, the 'me' claiming ownership of the thought is itself just a component of the thought. In truth, I do not even know what 'my' next thought will be until it occurs. In the words of Rumi, a 13th century Sufi poet:

Be empty of worrying.
*Think of who created thought!**

The *universal animating energy* is the One who creates thought. From this perspective the mind/brain is more the receiver than the generator of thought, comparable to a TV. Taking a television set apart will not reveal the source of the sounds and pictures. In the same way, we cannot find the thinker of thoughts inside the body-mind.

The animating energy – the One manifesting as the illusion of the many – is the source of everything, including all thoughts. It is not merely the thought 'I am,' but the absolute certainty of 'I Am.' This certainty is with you without your having to think about it. It stands on its own and is not limited to the 'I am' that's part of the various relative labels, such as I am a carpenter, a brother, a father, a mother, a friend, a daughter etc. The sense of identification with such temporary and relative labels is reflective of the Self's creation of the illusory ego.

*Play your part in the comedy, but don't identify yourself with your role!***

Ramana Maharshi recommended that one investigate by asking the question 'Who am I?' When asked who you are, there might be a hesitation as to what to answer; but when asked if you exist, there is no such doubt. The answer is a resounding, 'Yes, of course I exist.' When the answer to the first question is as clear as the answer to the second

---

* From *Why Lazurus Laughed* by Wei Wu Wei. Sentient Publications.
** From *The Essential Rumi* compiled and translated by Coleman Barks. Castle Books.

question, there is understanding.

The realization is that both questions have, in fact, the same answer. That which is sure of its existence – the innermost certainty of I Am – is what you essentially are. In other words: *I Am this knowing that knows that I Am.* The Hindus say Tat Tvam Asi (Thou Art That). In the Old Testament, God says, 'I Am that I Am.' This undeniable 'I Am' is not you in the personal sense, but the universal Self. Ramana Maharshi called the fundamental oneness of 'I Am' and the universal Self 'I-I.'

Watching from this understanding, I see how thoughts appear in 'my' awareness like clouds in a clear blue sky and then, without a trace, dissolve back in to it. Actually there's no need to proclaim that thoughts appear in *my* awareness; *in Awareness* suffices. Thoughts and everything else simply happen. Everything *is,* without a 'me' orchestrating it from behind the scenes. The ego is as non-essential to thinking or to the general functioning of the body-mind organism as Atlas is to supporting the heavens. And just as the ancient Greeks at some point realized that, in fact, there never was a titan named Atlas supporting the firmament, you can realize there never was an actual ego supporting the absolute certainty of 'I Am.'

There is no need to accept these words. You can investigate by looking inside and trying to locate a separate self. You will not find this 'ghost in the machine' that is supposed to be the thinker of your thoughts, the feeler of your feelings, and the doer of your deeds, except as a thought or a grammatical convention. You are that which is looking for this 'I,' and as long as the search continues, this will be overlooked.

This realization is a Copernican revolution removing

the ego from the center of the universe.* It is not, however, intended to be a new concept to hold on to. Ramana Maharshi compared a false concept to a thorn in your flesh. You can use another thorn (concept) to remove the first one; but afterward you throw both away. Holding onto the second one will, in time, result in your 'pricking' yourself again. The thorn in these very words is that they seem to suggest the existence of a 'you' that should let go of both thorns, while there is, in fact, no one to hold on to anything. The concept of the original I Am (pure being without the duality of someone being something) is just another signpost pointing at Pure Awareness; and like water that has no need of getting wet, Pure Awareness has no need of the thought 'I Am.' It is that.

I am the light that is above them all,
I am the All,
The All came forth from Me
and the All attained to me.
Cleave a piece of wood and I am there;
*Lift up a stone and you will find me there.***

---

* Nicolaus Copernicus (1473-1543) put forth the notion that the Sun, not the Earth, was the center of the solar system, radically upsetting the Middle Age worldview. In fact nothing changed, the Earth and the other planets did not move from their path, but the dominating point of view shifted, resulting in a much simpler and more elegant map of the heavens.

** From *The Gospel According to Thomas.* Harper & Row

11
Who is watching the show?

When a schoolteacher writes 'I' on a blackboard and asks the students what they see, most of them will answer that they see the word 'I.' It's rare for someone to say 'I see a blackboard with 'I' written on it.' Just as the relatively huge blackboard is ignored in favor of a single letter, we ignore the Awareness that is the permanent background to all phenomena. We tend to ignore this in the same way that we forget the screen on which a movie is projected. It is the unchanging characteristic in all the movies we watch, but it never gets involved in the movie, as such. The movie may depict an ocean, a long winding road, a murder, or a forest fire; but the screen will not get wet, move from place to place, bleed or burn. Likewise, Awareness remains pure and unaffected by its content.

Awareness is the consistent characteristic in and behind all experience, yet it is also that which most easily escapes our attention. Attention is not the same as Awareness. Our brain is designed in such a way that giving attention to something automatically implies ignoring something else. We see the stars and ignore the space; we read this text and ignore the page; we see the movie and ignore the screen; yet it is obvious that the ignored space, page, and screen are as fundamental to our observations as the stars, the text, and the movie, which hold our attention. This is an important point, as the mechanics of attention often get confused with Awareness. Attention works through noticing something in contrast to something that's ignored, while Awareness is the non-dual space that sustains both the noticed and the ignored. Attention may require effort; Awareness simply is. Everything that comes up is contained in and embraced by this Awareness, including objects perceived as 'out there' (rocks, cars, other sentient beings) and emotions, thoughts, and feelings experienced as 'in here.' In this sense, Awareness is as much in the body-mind as the body-mind is in Awareness. Compare it to a clay pot, which contains space and at the same time is contained by space. Breaking the pot will not affect this space.

In the same way, when the body-mind organism dies, nothing happens to Awareness. To see that you are this Awareness is to see that you were never born, never lived, and that you will never die. You *are* the living Awareness, which is the clear and open space in and from which everything arises, including your body-mind and your sense of individuality. No matter where you turn the spotlight of your attention, the floodlight of awareness is already there. It is aware of everything – of your breath going in and out, of the sudden sound, the light, and the falling of a sparrow halfway around the world. Pure Awareness is unconditioned and without attributes; it is simply present with no beginning or end, and it does not require any effort on your part. If you make an effort, Awareness is effortlessly aware of this. All that arises is its content, but this does not affect it any more than a mirror is affected by what it reflects. Like the mirror, Awareness makes no effort to accept or reject anything. It does not judge or take a point of view because it includes all possible points of view. The following poem attributed to the Taoist philosopher Chuang Tzu illustrates this.

The wild geese do not intend to cast their reflection:
The water has no mind to receive their image.*

It is only because of the dualistic and linear nature of language that this text appears to split that which is essentially one into Pure Awareness and its content. In reality, there is no such duality.

In this dualistic description, Awareness stands for the permanent, while the appearances in Awareness represent the impermanent; but really they are the two sides of a single coin. However, to speak of two sides is still using two labels for one indefinable something. Perhaps it's a better metaphor to say that the height of the mountain *is* the depth of the valley.

Pure Awareness does not need anything other than itself to be what it is. Contrary to what logic dictates, it does not need an object outside of itself to be aware of. Another way of saying this is that Awareness is both the subject *and* the object. As such Awareness is Self-luminous. It is a Self-sustaining, Self-aware feedback loop, which the use of language seems to split into subject/object, the creator and the created, or Awareness and its content. The Hindus illustrate this with the image of a spider, which produces a web from its own body, plays in it and then draws it back into itself.

The Self is producing, watching, and appearing in and as the grand show of the unfolding cosmic drama, just as

---
* From *The way of Zen* by Alan Watts. Vintage

a dreamer simultaneously produces, watches, and appears in her dream. You, me, the book, the chair, and the terrorists on the news are all variations in the way Awareness appears to itself, just as the people, the house, the sunrise, and the monsters appearing in a dream are all made of the same dream stuff.

In the audience aspect of itself, Awareness is referred to as *the witness,* the one who is watching the show.

12
The shift

Perhaps you're familiar with the concept of the witness. The witness is recognized by a shift in the center of gravity, from the temporal content of Awareness to Pure Awareness itself, from the concept of identifying as a separate personal ego to the clear and open space in which feelings, thoughts, and everything else effortlessly arises. In a sense, this witnessing is upstream from your thoughts and feelings, although assigning it a location in space and time is impossible. It is always right at the center and simultaneously underlies and oversees all phenomena. Witnessing is often suddenly glimpsed and then apparently lost again. Such a glimpse may feel somewhat like the surprised and uncertain feeling one gets when first riding a bicycle. 'Hey I'm doing it!' As you may have discovered, this thought often makes you lose your balance.

The impersonal witness cannot itself be witnessed, just as the eye cannot directly see itself. The witness is aware of – and prior to – all thoughts, including the thought that there is an individual to do the witnessing. That is why identifying with the 'I' in the thought, 'Now I've got it!' is the return of the illusory 'me.' We could call it a shift in the center of gravity from the witness back to the ego, or from identifying with Awareness to identifying with its content. It is, however, only an apparent shift, following from the thought, 'Now I've got it!' We are so used to the grammatical structure of the thought process – which divides thinking into a thinker and his thoughts – that we forget that the 'I' (or ego) is itself part of the thought stream. The thought 'Now I've got it!' includes the 'I' that supposedly *got* some separate 'it.' Because this 'I' is itself part of the stream of thought, it can never quite get at the witness of this stream. At the same time, beyond the ego illusion, you *are* the indefinable, ungraspable witness, seeing the coming and going of all thoughts – including the 'I' in 'Now I've got it.' This I, or ego, is often thought of as a conscious entity. In reality the ego is not conscious, but the witness is conscious of the ego.

We have to be alert here. It's easy to forget that, when talking or thinking about it, even the witness is turned into a concept and, as such, a part of the witnessed stream of thought. It is a subtle concept, but a concept nevertheless. Misunderstood as the middle ground between the concept of Pure Awareness and that of the ego, it can become a trap when used as an excuse to dissociate from one's feelings and daily experiences. 'Oh it's not me who's in a lousy mood, I am only observing it.' When we use the concept of the witness to avoid feeling the pain of the mood and attempt to change it into a mood we like, we are again identified with an 'I' that wants things to be different from the way they are, hence reinforcing the idea that there really is such an independent 'I.'

Witnessing is not something we progress to. It is not about self-improvement or mental states. It is about recognizing that which is already fully present; this presence observes both the 'I' and its states while, at the same time, it remains unaffected. If we see this witnessing as a new way to make us feel good, we are back at square one. Instead of identifying with the conceptual ego, we have now identified with the conceptual witness – still an independent, identified entity, merely in different garb. From this more cushioned perspective, it's easy to get trapped again in the same old illusion. As soon as the witness has become an object or concept, it becomes part of the witnessed. The real witness will never be an object of experience, but always remains that which is aware of the experience. Objectified, it becomes the 'new ego;' non-objectified, it merges with Pure Awareness – that which we so intimately are that we cannot get at it; like an arrow, able to point in all directions, but not at itself.

All these words may make us forget that the actuality of Pure Awareness is not an abstraction, nor something remote, but the very essence of this, as it is. We are totally intimate with it, to the extent that it is more accurate to say that we are it: It is our true being. It is open, clear, and present, and yet, it evades all attempts from the mind to capture it in conceptual structures.

Perhaps we can clarify this apparent paradox by putting it next to something we all directly know: Space. Three dimensional space is all around us. It cannot be said to have locality yet it allows for everything to have a location. We see it everywhere, but we cannot describe how it looks. It has no taste, shape, color, or substance. It cannot be cut, damaged, or taken hold of, and yet we know it intimately as that in which everything appears. The same holds true for Awareness. You, being this space-like Awareness, are not in the world, but the world and all that exists is in you.

Sri Nisargadatta Maharaj puts it beautifully:

You see yourself in the world while I see the world in myself. To you, you get born and die, while to me, the world appears and disappears. *

The 'I,' Maharaj refers to is obviously not the separate impermanent self that Alan Watts has called 'the skin encapsulated ego.' Rather, it is the intimate mystery of the impersonal Self that lives and manifests as all that is. It is the One Without a Second, the witness that cannot be witnessed, and the knower that cannot be known.

In the preface of the first edition of Sri Krishna Menon's Atma Darshan I found the following description:

Living beings perceive objects by the light of the sun. This makes them superimpose upon the sun the function of illuminating objects. In the same way thoughts and objects reveal themselves in consciousness. When the function of revealing is superimposed upon consciousness it becomes the witness. As a mater of fact consciousness shines of itself. Light or revelation is its very nature, not its function or property.**

You truly are this consciousness! As always throughout this text, you are encouraged to take this literally: If there is only One, then that is all there is, and you can only be *that* – not a part (apart) of it, but IT! Do not be bamboozled by the magical illusion of the moon reflected in a thousand lakes. It is still only one moon. Similarly, do not get hypnotized by the illusion of multiplicity. It is still the one Self, which only *appears* as the many: A

---

* From *I Am That*. Chetana Publications, Mumbai, India
** From *Atma Darshan*. Sri Atmananda Krishna Menon. Sri Vidya Samiti

No-thing-ness that witnesses, reflects, generates, destroys, contains, sustains, and *is* this manifestation.

13
No claim, no blame, no fame

As I am sitting at my computer writing these words, I become aware of the sensation of thirst. Simultaneously comes the thought, 'A cup of tea would be nice.' This all happens spontaneously without me first deciding to be thirsty and then to think of tea.

If you watch your mind, you will see that thoughts arise of their own accord. Please, do not simply accept or reject this. When you honestly observe and investigate, it will become clear that you are not the thinker of your thoughts. What this chapter will try to show is that you are also not the doer of your deeds. This may go against your deepest convictions and beliefs, so I ask you to suspend the judgment that may come up as a reflex and see what is really being offered here.

All apparent decisions and choices are thoughts. To act upon a thought feels like choice and is labeled choice by the language, but choice is really just the expression of whatever thought arises most predominantly. I did not choose my desire for tea, nor did I choose the stronger desire that I should finish the paragraph first, but that is what is spontaneously happening. This is not to say that I am an apparatus without free will. There is actually no individual here to be deprived of free will. The thought of 'I' and the thoughts of tea and typing merely unfold as a manifestation of the animating energy of Pure Awareness.

From this perspective, there is a sense that life is simply living, thinking, and acting through you and as you. The Taoists call this Wu Wei, which loosely translates as *non-doing*. This does not mean doing nothing in the sense of inertia, but rather that everything – including 'your' thoughts and actions – is happening naturally and of its own accord. Lao Tsu describes it in the *Tao Te Ching* as follows:

> *Tao, without doing anything,*
> *Leaves nothing undone (37)*

And again:
> *Less and less is done,*
> *Till only non-action remains.*
> *Nothing is done, yet nothing is left undone. (48)*

In Buddha's words:
> *Suffering exists, but none who suffer,*
> *The deed there is, but no doer thereof.*

We all know the feeling of being in the flow of things. At such times, we lose ourselves in our activity. Writers frequently have this experience when the words seem to simply pour onto the page and they have no idea what the next line is going to be until they write it. Most athletes also have moments when suddenly everything clicks and they manage to perform beyond their normal capacity. There are sometimes moments during lovemaking when lovers melt into a union that knows no separate individuality.

Or what about narrowly averted accidents on the highway where you later wonder just who was steering the car? I'm sure if you think about it, you have had several such experiences in which you forgot yourself and everything seemed to magically fall into place.

This forgetfulness is very different from forgetting your friend's birthday or where you put your glasses. Nor is it like the absentmindedness induced by too much booze or too many tranquilizers. It is a forgetfulness that is alert and alive. This losing oneself in the flow is a taste of what is meant by 'the action of non-action.'

All works are being done by the Gunas (or the energy and power) of nature, but due to delusion of ego, people assume themselves to be the doer. (3.27)*

Although being in the flow feels wonderful, the idea of our actions happening by themselves instead of through our free will can be upsetting. This is especially true for the western mind, which tends to view free will as either an inherent quality of one's prized individuality or a gift/test from God to see if one is strong enough to do the right thing. For the atheist, his doing or failing to do the right thing may be a measure of his true character; for the religious person there is a lot more at stake, since for him it determines the quality of his after-life.

From the free will point of view, the idea that something is living through us can be quite objectionable. It seems to reduce us to mere marionettes, implying a helplessness, which is hard to accept. Furthermore, there arises a fear that if nothing we do is truly our own action, then

* From *The Bhagavad-Gita* translated by Dr. Ramanand Prasad

people have an excuse for undesirable behavior. What is overlooked in such arguments is that *all* activity is of the one Self, appearing as the multiplicity of characters that apparently do the thinking, acting, and choosing. To excuse our undesirable behavior on these grounds does not work, for there will still be consequences. You may protest that the thought that led you to steal from your employer simply arose, and you are not responsible; but then neither is your employer responsible for the thought that led him to fire you and press charges.

Ultimately, since the ego is an illusion, it cannot be deprived of free will nor can it be the victim of predestination. The ego is neither the doer nor the non-doer; it simply does not have an existence independent of the Self, any more than a character in a novel exists independently of the author who portrays him. He and all other characters in the story arise from the imagination of the writer. When it is realized that we all arise from Pure Awareness in much the same way, it is instantly clear that there is no one from whom free will could have been taken. The moment the ego's point of view gets dropped, there is the liberating realization of a divine energy spontaneously manifesting as us. There's then no one left to experience a sense of helplessness, and it is clearly seen that the helplessness is just another thought.

Like St. Paul said:

I live, yet not I, but Christ - the eternal Logos - liveth in me. (Gal 2:20).

The paradox in the suggestion that the ego should be dropped is that when one is not the doer, one cannot do the dropping. What happens is more like a falling away, which comes in its own time and which is nothing other than the impersonal recognition of the ego's illusory nature. Although this realization comes by itself – it is often referred to as grace – it is not something one has to wait for. Waiting is just another way of trying to get it, which only perpetuates the illusion that there really is *someone* who should get *something*.

Intellectually accepting the idea that we should not try often results in trying not to try. This is what in psychology is called the double bind or in everyday language, 'damned if you do and damned if you don't.'

This double bind is acutely felt when you try to will yourself to forget something unpleasant. It also features prominently in so-called self-improvement projects and can lead to bizarre thought patterns such as:

I will correct my habit of correcting myself and others;
I will no longer put up with intolerance;
I'll put a real effort into becoming more relaxed; and
I can hardly wait to become more patient.
I will really try to be more spontaneous;
I will seriously work on my sense of humor; and
In the very near future, I resolve to become more accepting of what is right now.

Okay, this might be a slight exaggeration, but it shows the principle at work through the contradictions that pop up when the ego embarks on a project of becoming better adjusted, more accepting, or more relaxed. As long as we believe that there is an ego to either improve or remove, and as long as we work toward the betterment or elimination of that ego, the more the illusion is perpetuated. It's like looking in the mirror and seeing your face. Trying to remove your face by cleaning the mirror is useless. If you simply walk away, it's not there anymore; but you don't see that. All you know is that every time you look it's still there, and you may decide that more cleaning is needed. During the course of the day we often 'forget' to look and, in such moments, we are totally without a sense of ego. We don't realize this since during these moments there is no 'I' to notice its absence.

The deceptive sense of a personal self is a complex system of thoughts, memories (a special kind of thoughts), emotions and conditioning. This mental structure may even cause certain sensations in the body-mind, through, for example, habitual muscular contractions and nerve firings, further supporting the perception of the illusion as reality. We may argue that when it is felt and perceived it also must exist. It's fine to take that position, but then realize that the ego illusion is not so much in what we label as the ego, as in our identification with it. In the same way, we could say that a mirage of an oasis in the desert exists when it is observed; or we could say that it does not. It only becomes a problem when it is not recognized for what it truly is and one expects to find water there.

See that you are not limited to this mirage known as the ego. You are that which appears as and − at the same time − is aware of the ego. The ego concept is built into the very syntax we use for thinking and talking. Thinking 'I have an ego' is just a thought; but so is thinking 'I don't have an ego.' Both thoughts include 'I' along with 'ego,' and both appear and disappear again without leaving a trace on the mirror of Pure Awareness. Stop looking, and it's gone.

When a student asked Sri Atmananda, 'When will I get it?' he answered, 'When the *when* stops.' Normally the mind then asks 'And when will that be?' The answer can only be 'Right here and right now!' This literally means that you do not have to wait for grace to set you free. You already are free. Saying that you do not have to wait for this freedom is not meant to put you again into a double bind, in which you might try to give up trying or find yourself waiting for the waiting to stop. It's just a reminder that the silent space of Pure Awareness already is. It sees and contains the reading of these words and the arising of thoughts, which then are identified as 'your' thoughts. It is in and prior to the energizing of your senses and available as everything that's presenting itself at this very instant. The acceptance of this reveals what you truly are. Behind the veil of ignorance (ignore-ance), you *are* the Awakened One, aware of – as well as appearing in and as – this marvelous show of manifestation. You are, at once, Awareness and the totality of its content.

Again, let me stress that, due to the limitations of language, I seem to suggest that there is Awareness on one hand and its content on the other. In truth, there is nothing but Oneness here, preceding and including the duality of duality and non-duality. There is no individual entity to either get it or not get it; there is only *this*. There is not now, nor was there ever, an ego either to be burdened by guilt or to bask in individual glory. No claim, no blame, no shame, and no fame – it all goes out of the window when thoughts, feelings, decisions, and actions are known as arising spontaneously from the welter of life.

If you cannot believe this and are still convinced that you are a separate individual in charge of your life, try this small experiment. Right now in this moment decide to feel elation and feel it. Then think of your least favorite food and for the next five minutes really crave it. Consider your opinion on capital punishment and change it. Finally, ask yourself what your next thought will be and see if you can know it in advance. While you're busy doing this or perhaps hosting a thought stream that rejects it as nonsense, the divine play of life magically unfolds by itself.

You will find that when your claim on thoughts, feelings, and actions dissolves, your ability to deal with the day-to-day business of living doesn't get impaired. On the contrary, it becomes less stressful. When the person you thought you were continues as a dreamed character – as one of the many guises of the universal actor – there is no longer any effort dedicated to keeping up appearances, no need to carry resentment, no point in worrying about an imaginary future.

To sum it up, thinking that you're no more than your limited role is buying into the illusion; realizing that you're the one actor playing all the roles is liberation.

In this context, it is interesting to note that the word *person* comes from the masks that were used in ancient Greek-Roman theatre. Per-sona: Through (per) which the sound (sona) is coming.

14

To practice or not to practice

The former chapter on doership/non-doership may leave you with questions about spiritual practice. Is there a place for it? Can it lead to freedom, enlightenment, or Self-realization, or is there no point to it at all?

First of all I want to say that whatever arises for you is appropriate. It is as it is and, as such, it is the way the Self appears in this moment. Now, in this moment it is appropriate for you to read these words, and they will have whatever effect they will.

Although this chapter focuses mainly on meditation, what is said here applies to spiritual practice in general.

If you are an avid practitioner of meditation – especially if you have made a big investment of time and effort in hopes that this approach will lead to enlightenment – you may not like what you're going to read. Perhaps you have spent a lot of money on books and classes. As a writer of such books or a teacher of such classes, you could even depend on meditation for your livelihood.

If you did make a hefty investment in this practice with the intention to find enlightenment, it will take courage and an open mind to absorb what's being offered here. It is not meant as a judgment or as discouragement; but it invites you to take a shortcut to Self-realization, right here and right now. Remember, by Self-realization I do not mean something you have to get or attain. After all, there is a reason it has been labeled Self-realization instead of Self-improvement, Self-attainment, or Self-acquirement. Self-realization means simply to recognize what you already and truly are.

As a practice, meditation can lead to relaxation, changed brain waves, and altered states of mind. As such, it can play a part in healing and can deliver marvelous experiences; but these are not what Self-realization is about. Nor is it about the 'I' that has, remembers, and interprets the experiences. If Self-realization is about anything, it is about the aware space in which both the illusion of the separate 'I' and its experiences occur. Meditation – or any other spiritual practice for that matter – can never lead to what is. This reminds me of a story about Chan master Ma-Tsu (709-789).

> *One day Ma-Tsu's master found him meditating and asked, 'What are you doing here?'*
>
> *Ma-Tsu replied, 'I am meditating to attain Buddha-hood.'*
>
> *The master sat next to him, picked up a stone and started polishing it.*
>
> *Ma-Tsu asked what he was doing.*
>
> *The master responded, 'I am making a mirror.'*
>
> *'No' Ma-Tsu cried out, 'It cannot be done this way.'*
>
> *'Similarly, you cannot become a Buddha by sitting in meditation,' retorted the master.*

If meditation is happening, then that is what is, and there is nothing wrong with it – especially if you take pleasure in it the same way you might enjoy dancing or listening to music. Like those activities, meditation generates whatever benefits it generates.

A student of meditation may have come to see his true nature, but this clarity has also come to many who never meditated in a formal sense. The mistake comes when people have a mystical experience through meditation, confuse this with enlightenment, and then teach others to meditate in order to get similarly enlightened. Enlightenment is not an experience, nor is it the result of a progressive path via which one comes ever closer to the desired goal. Such a progressive path may consist of rigorous practice and discipline, but to discipline and restrict yourself in order to be free is futile. It is an attempt to get rid of attempting, an action taken to arrive at non-action, which has as its motive to become pure and free of motives.

On the other hand, meditation purely for the love of meditation is an expression of joy. It can happen everywhere, at any moment, and is not limited to a specific hour of the day where one sits in a specific posture and follows the breath or repeats a mantra. It is not needy, but is an ongoing openness to, and celebration of, the ever-present silent space of Awareness. In truth, you already are this Awareness, and you do not have to work to become what you already are. The only thing that blocks your seeing this right now is your insistence that you're not *there* yet, that you need to work, to purify or discipline yourself in order to reach 'the promised land of enlightenment.'

So I went on practicing very hard. I did zazen. I went and lived in the mountains. I disciplined myself as severely as

* From *The Unborn - The Life and Teachings of Zen Master Bankei* (1622 – 1693) Translated by Norman Waddell. North Point Press

I possibly could. But none of it helped a bit. I didn't get any closer to understanding the Buddha-mind.

If you could just STOP, you'd realize that you're already there – or rather HERE. At this ever present still point it is impossible to distinguish between meditation and simple being. To accept this is to understand why seeking and working on your self are not helping at all. You can become professional at spiritual practice; and you can get stuck in seeking, thereby affirming that this, *as it is*, is somehow incomplete and in need of your efforts to fix and improve it.

Reading this, the following question may arise: 'Is there then absolutely nothing that can be done? Do we just have to sit, wait, and hope for things to become clear?' The answer is that waiting for clarity still assumes a separate identity as a reality and sees awakening into Awareness as locked away in an imaginary future. If there is anything at all to do, it is to verify in this instant the truth of what you are; to confirm that Awareness is fully present and that no effort is required for this to be so.

This inquiry will show that meditating to become enlightened is as counterproductive as fighting for peace. Each effort confirms and reinforces the illusion that there really is a separate entity that is *not there* yet. Clearly, the timeless does not start later on, nor is the ever-present on its way, scheduled for arrival at some point in the future. It is present right here and right now. When I say 'here and now' I do not mean the fleeting moment between past and future, but the eternal present, which contains the apparent flux of time. Now, in this moment, I am writing these words; and now, in this moment, you are reading them. You may make a great effort to be fully here and now, but even if you wanted to, could you be anywhere else? Even when you take your mind for a walk down memory lane, get caught up in fantasies, or anticipate some future event, you are here and now. Ask yourself how many steps it takes to get to where you are? How much time does it take to arrive at this moment? How much effort is required to be what you already are?

For the dedicated seeker, this may seem too simple, if not simplistic. He likes to work on things and to feel that he is making progress. He likes systems and linear approaches. Meditation as a practice to achieve enlightenment, insight, or peace, may seem to be just the ticket. The seeker may identify formal meditation, with its long esoteric tradition, as a valid tool with which to realize his objectives. He anticipates the pride of accomplishment and the glory of personal achievement. 'Look mom, no ego!'

Again, I want to remind the seeker of the paradox he creates when going after total freedom and realization. His activity of formal meditation, or any other spiritual practice for that matter, is arising *in* totality and, consequently, cannot lead *to* totality. The intellectually inclined seeker, who depends on the mind's dualistic approach to solving problems, figuring out methods, and grasping concepts, finds the slippery slope of non-duality especially frustrating territory. He knows, but at some point he may see that he can never know the knower. He can think about this 'problem,' but in the process, he turns the knower into a concept and finds that, just as it seems about to be grasped, it has changed again into the known. The knower is forever beyond knowing. Because of the dualistic approach by which the mind is trying to get at this knower, the seeker finds himself in a position comparable to someone who is turning around and around in a fruitless attempt to observe his own back.

> *The nature of phenomena is nondual,*
> *but each one, in its own state,*
> *is beyond the limits of the mind.*
> *There is no concept that can define*
> *the condition of 'what is'*
> *but vision nevertheless manifests: all is good.*
> *Everything has already been accomplished,*
> *and so, having overcome the sickness of effort,*
> *one finds oneself in the self-perfected state:*
> *this is contemplation.**

The intellect finds true meditation – which is not a quest for understanding, being, or silence, but the understanding, being and silence itself – forever beyond its reach. The simple realization of *what is* cannot be an achievement, but is instantly seen when the 'I' and the 'want' are taken out of the I-want-realization-approach.

Another way of seeing this is to follow your path backward. Instead of going after the realization you want, look to where the want arises; then take another step back and observe from where the 'I' arises. What is the silence before the 'I'? What is this no-thing-ness, this absolute presence? Does it strive to get something or somewhere? Does it need to become something, or does all becoming arise from and in it?

Formal meditation may spin a mantra around the brain

* From *Dzogchen: The Self-Perfected State* by Chogyal Namkhai Norbu. Snow Lion Publications

to silence the continuous stream of thoughts; but in true meditation, thoughts are seen to occur freely and are not viewed as problematic interruptions that need to be controlled by an imaginary ego claiming to be bothered by them. The key here is to see that this ego is itself part of the stream of thought it wants to control and that it has no reality independent of thought. Clearly, there is no need for this ghostly helmsman of an ego to steer the mind to a single point of concentration. All is freely arising and welcomed, including mantras, the ego illusion, thoughts and emotions. None of this activity is able to affect the silent space of Pure Awareness in which it has its moment and – without leaving a trace – dissolves.

> *Meditation is not a way to enlightenment, nor is it a method of achieving anything at all.*
> *It is peace itself.*
> *It is the actualization of wisdom, the ultimate truth of the oneness of all things.**

---

* Dogen (1200-1253 AD). Founder of the Soto Zen lineage.

15

Acceptance, unconditional love, bliss, and all this

Acceptance, unconditional love and bliss are magical words well known by most travelers on the spiritual path. Like most words, their nature is somewhat ambiguous. They are inviting and, at the same time, create huge expectations. These are things we want, but which, at the same time, may well look unattainable.

As a child, I remember being told that the way to catch a bird was to put salt on its tail. I was too young to realize that if I could do this, I would have already caught the bird. The same sort of paradox is inherent in the concepts talked about in this chapter. For example, we cannot arrive at total acceptance by trying to change things. This trying implies that we do not accept the way it is. When the trying is abandoned there is total acceptance and the bird is already caught. Seekers often ignore this paradox and keep trying in the hope or belief that if one manages to totally accepts what is, Self-realization will follow and, as a consequence, one will know unconditional love and bliss.

This whole universe is the dream of the Self. Our identity is a conceptual reference point on a continuum that is the deep Self, and when we use words like unconditional love, bliss, and acceptance, we are reaching for our own hands.

As mentioned above, there is a belief amongst seekers that acceptance can lead to Self-realization, clarity, and, ultimately, enlightenment. The truth is that the 'me' trying to be accepting can never catch this bird. Total acceptance is what is right here and right now – not something that one can accomplish in the future. Acceptance does not lead to clarity; it *is* the clarity that whatever is cannot be different in any way. Things might apparently be different then they *were*, but they can never be different then they *are*. All efforts to become more accepting, loving, or blissful are only the illusion of the ego attempting to validate itself as a real player that can progress toward increasingly refined states of being.

Pure Awareness does not actively practice acceptance, love, and bliss as the polar opposites of rejection, hate, and despair. This would not qualify as *total* acceptance. Pure Awareness is like a mirror that reflects everything without the least resistance. All is accepted without the slightest judgment. This includes how you appear to yourself right now. Get this: It includes your fat, your bald spot, your anger, your doubts, your alienation, and your fear, as well as all the warm fuzzy stuff. Whether there is resistance, rejection, striving or straining doesn't matter. All this is witnessed and thereby accepted.

Being the one Self, forever perfect and all-pervasive, what would I accept and what would I reject, what would give me joy and what would give me sorrow? Being ever unaffected and unattached I am at peace in my unfathomable Self.*

---

* From *Self-Realization* Compiled and edited by Al Drucker. Atma Press

Acceptance, or the clarity of what you are, will not come as a result of your efforts or seeking, but may be revealed when the trying and seeking drops away. Then, total acceptance, love, and bliss could be recognized as being already here. Self-realization or Self-recognition – which simply means seeing what you already are right this instant – equals total acceptance. Can 'you' accept that there is nothing to do? Can 'you' accept that you do not exist as a separate entity? If you can, then who is left to *do* the accepting?

Whether the thought that arises says 'this is accepted' or whether it says, 'this is not accepted' makes no difference. Pure Awareness includes – and thereby accepts – both.

The ego is not capable of total acceptance, but is included in it. It hopes in vain that, through its efforts to become more and more accepting, it will reach the exalted state of enlightenment. This, in turn, is expected to result in eternal bliss, peace, and the experience of unconditional love. This prize the ego is after is, however, not an experience one can have, nor is it a state that one can be in. On the contrary, enlightenment is the evaporation of the illusion that there is an individual to experience it, which is why it has been called the 'stateless state.'

Total acceptance, unconditional love, and bliss are in fact just three more pointers to the clear space of Pure Awareness from which the pointing is done – the realm beyond zero and one. In this purity, without qualifications or form, even the concepts of the witness and the witnessed, of the mirror and its content, must dissolve.

We may call it bliss, as nothing can disturb it.

We may call it total acceptance, as nothing is rejected by it.

We may call it unconditional love, as everything is embraced by it.

This magnificent simplicity, this open secret, this intimate clarity is all there is. It is yourself welcoming you home. *You are this.*

16
What about the body?

So far, we have mostly ignored the body. What about it? Is it just a piece of meat? Is it our temple, a toy, a tool, or a burden? Depending on our health, age, and conditioning, it could be each or any combination of those. In this chapter and the next one, we will take a look at the body and what happens to us when it dies.

We see the body as a solid object, but a closer inspection reveals the exact opposite. It breaks down into bones and soft tissue, which break down into cells. If we keep zooming in, we come to atoms – the building blocks for everything in the universe – consisting of mainly empty space. These atoms have relatively huge distances between them, comparable to those we find between the stars. If all the atoms that make up your body were compressed into the smallest possible space, they would barely amount to the size of a pinhead. These atoms can be reduced to subatomic particles, which break up into energy/nothingness. So the apparent concrete reality of the body turns out to dissolve into space, yet, magically, it is experienced as a solid object.

As a seeker, you probably have heard more than once that you are not the body; as for example in the following quote:

I am not the body,
Nor is the body mine.
*I am awareness itself.**

The major religions seem to agree that the body is a temporary vehicle for an individual's immortal essence, or soul. Many people say they believe this; but when it comes down to it, heaven can wait, and funerals are generally occasions for sadness rather than joy. While claiming to adhere to the view of being an immortal soul in a mortal body, most of us do, in fact, identify with and experience ourselves as the body. We can hear this in how we talk about ourselves. For example: I am tired, I am strong, I am ill, I am born and I will die.

The body's capacity for pain and pleasure puts us on a quest for security and gratification. Identification with the body combined with the perception of time leads us to the belief in our mortality. We project our hopes and fears into the future and run after anything we imagine we need. It may be peace and security, status and comfort, or love and recognition. However, our striving has an unwelcome twin brother called fear. In other words, hoping that one will get something is the nice way of saying that one is afraid of not getting it. Even when we are on the positive trip of making something out of our lives, we get to deal with the negative implications of this approach. For example, when we attempt to improve ourselves or our life's circumstances, we are in fact, saying that we want things to be different. Consequently, this implies that at some level we are not happy with the way things are.

---

* *The Heart of Awareness* (11-6) a translation of the Ashtavakra Gita by Thomas Byrom. Shambhala Publications

The dominant culture on our planet encourages us to strive for constant growth and improvement, which can create a persistent feeling that this, *as it is*, is not sufficient; that this is *not* it. People who do not conform to this view are scoffed at and seen as fatalists or lacking in drive and ambition. Such a 'the only way is up attitude' is in direct opposition to the cyclic way nature expresses itself. The ebb and flood of the oceans, the waxing and waning of the moon, the four seasons, and birth and dying are just a few examples.

When buying into the 'constant linear progress myth,' we may frantically work on becoming a better person and/or having a better future. In spite of our best efforts, we often find that life does not unfold as planned and that, even when we get exactly what we want, the anticipated pleasure is temporary at best. Over and over, the new thing becomes the old thing and, as the moment of pleasure passes, we once again start looking for the next new thing. Sri Atmananda pointed out that the pleasure one experiences on achieving a goal or acquiring an object of desire is wrongly ascribed to such an achievement or acquisition. The joy does not come from fulfilling the desire, but causeless joy, which is our true nature, shines unobstructed when we are momentarily without desire.

We've all heard the saying 'Be careful what you wish for,' implying that getting what you want often has unanticipated side effects. Most of us would love to win the lottery, but it is well known that many lottery winners have ended up unhappy, with a whole set of new and unforeseen problems. Both getting what we desire and not getting it can turn out to be a disappointment. It is the very nature of desire to be unfulfilled, and consequently even a 'good' desire, such as the desire for peace, will keep us from the peace we seek.

Generally, suffering comes from the dualistic outlook in which the assumed difference between a conceptual me and the world of apparent objects generates desire and fear. More specifically related to our identification with the body, suffering originates in the belief that we are impermanent and mortal individuals. We see our body age or fall ill and, from our identified condition, we think that *we* are aging or falling ill.

The body's existence is a process in time, and our wish for its continuation is nothing but the fear of our own extinction. We tend to equate the body's survival with our own survival, and generally spend a lot of effort to prolong its existence. Strangely, many of us ignore our health and general well-being in the process, sometimes literally working ourselves to death. Even when we have much more than we had last year, we still may feel that we don't have enough. Of course, the future where we once and for all find ultimate security never arrives. Striving for it is like a donkey trying to reach the carrot that the rider on its back dangles in front of its nose. Both carrot and future recede as fast as they are approached. The irony here is that the future we work toward brings us ever closer to the death we fear. Often there is little appreciation that all there is is the present perfection of *this as it is*. If we just stop for a moment, relax, and simply be present, there may arise the recognition of life as timeless presence. To stop does not mean that we should become recluses or just stay in bed all day and do nothing. It means that we see through the illusion of being a time-bound mortal individual driven by fear and desire. Subsequently, our actions don't come from stress and striving, and we no longer perceive ourselves as individual doers. We can live fully in the certainty that this unique moment is complete, perfect, and its own reward.

To embrace the body's mortality without making it 'your' mortality is a liberating prospect. When you stop buying into the illusion that you are nothing but a body, fears about mortality and vulnerability, which can have the effect of spoiling the life you so dearly want to hang onto, dissolve. At this point, tension releases and is replaced with an appreciation of the natural flow of life. Things are 'done' for their own sake. Action is play and play is action.

To stop identifying with the body does not automatically imply that you become insensitive. It still hurts when you stub your toe, and there will still be unpleasant consequences if you neglect your health. It doesn't neutralize all feelings to a gray indifference, but allows them to arise and dissolve naturally. Labeling certain experiences, thoughts, and emotions as negative or positive may slow down, as well as the clinging to so-called 'positive' occurrences and the running from 'negative' ones. In this 'allowing' is freedom. The full spectrum of emotions and thoughts can still arise but will not refer to an illusionary 'me' residing inside a body. Pain can come up, but resistance will not compound it. Pleasure can occur, but will not be spoiled by attempts to hold onto it. Your true and eternal Self sees the body as one of many temporal appearances. How different this is from identifying with a perspective that sees the body's changes, such as aging, falling ill, and eventually dying, as happening to you.

The body is confined
By its natural properties.
It comes, It lingers awhile, It goes.
But the Self neither comes nor goes.
*So why grieve for the body?**

When we clearly see that all desire and its resulting suffering originates in the belief that there is a separate individual identified with a body-mind, we may be more receptive to the view that we are not the body.

The body is false,
And so are its fears,
Heaven and hell, freedom and bondage.
It is all invention.
What can they matter to me?
*I am awareness itself.**

The trick is to refrain from turning this notion into yet another strategy to escape undesirable moods and the fear of extinction. Believing or hoping that one is not the body usually gets translated into the idea that one is an immortal soul temporarily confined in the body; but this is not what this text suggests. What it says is that you are not exclusively the body in the same way that the ocean is not exclusively a single wave. You have identified with this mortal and time-bound appearance to the extent that you have apparently forgotten the bigger picture.

The bigger picture is that the body-mind is the infinite having a finite experience. You *are* the infinite, and the

---

* *The Heart of Awareness* (15-9 & 2-20) a translation of the Ashtavakra Gita by Thomas Byrom. Shambhala Publications

body resides in you the same way that a star resides in space. Realizing that you truly are the eternal space beyond birth, existence, and dying makes it clear that all temporal manifestations – including the body, experiences, thoughts, feelings, the grass, the trees, your next door neighbor, the saint, the terrorist, John in the next cubicle, and the politician on the evening news – appear in or against this background: Let me say this again: You are this background together with what appears against it. You are the unity of the eternal and the temporal; you are the One Without a Second.

The invitation extended here is to have this sense of being a separate individual melt back into the oceanic Self and to break free from the illusion of *exclusive* identification with the temporal body-mind. Simply *be* and know yourself once again in your true splendor, free from the illusory chains of birth and dying.

Because you think you are the body,
For a long time you have been bound.
Know you are pure awareness.
With this knowledge as your sword
Cut through your chains.
*And be happy!**

---

* *The Heart of Awareness* (1-14) a translation of the Ashtavakra Gita by Thomas Byrom. Shambhala Publications

17

Giving up the ghost

Death is not extinguishing the light;
*it is putting out the lamp because dawn has come.**

Death is certainly one of the greatest mysteries of life. Because it is an event horizon we cannot look beyond, it is a topic of speculation and of fear and fascination. Before we continue, we have to make an important distinction: The fear of dying is *not* the same as the fear of death. The former is a very practical and commonsense characteristic of the body, while the latter is a curious mix of fantasy and make-believe belonging to the mind. Animals know the fear of dying, but are, as far as we know, unfamiliar with the conceptual fear of death.

The fear of dying is that which stops you from disembarking an airborne plane without a parachute or from organizing a picnic on a train track. The fear of death, on the other hand, is more abstract as the mind projects a future in which it no longer exists. You could say that it mourns its own demise in advance. It terrifies itself with pictures of life being terminated, followed by an abyss of eternal nothingness and then recoils from this void as if

---
*Rabindranath Tagore (1861-1941) Indian/Bengali poet, novelist, educator, who won the Nobel Prize for Literature in 1913

nonexistence could be some kind of an experience; something like being buried alive in a cold and dark emptiness that goes on forever.

Ironically, the clinging to life can get in the way of living fully so that, in a round about way, the fear of dying becomes a fear of living. This fear comes at the cost of many of life's simple pleasures. For example, when riding a bicycle, protective clothing and helmets may add to our safety, but they definitely do not contribute to the pleasure of a leisurely tour through the countryside; taking care for one's health is a good thing, but it can become a restrictive obsession; making a living can turn into an ever accelerating struggle leading to stress, nervous-breakdowns, or worse.

Mortal fear is at the core of various religious belief systems, which offer the prospect of reincarnation or an after-life; but *is* there actually something beyond this life? If we take a good look at this question, we see it is predicated upon the assumption that there is, in fact, an individual that has been born and eventually will die.

If you believe that you are the body, then death seems an absolute certainty. If you believe that you are a soul residing in a body, then you assume your body dies, while that which is essentially 'you' survives. Surviving 'the crash' may seem great at first, but it's risky. Depending on your belief, there's always the chance of being assigned an 'inferior vehicle' next time around; or you may not qualify for the grand prize of Heaven and, instead, end up in eternal flames. All this, however, is a matter of belief/hope/fear and not a matter of knowing. Both the hope for an afterlife and the fear of death originate in the mistaken belief that you are a time-bound and mortal individual whose candle will be snuffed out when the grim reaper comes to get you. The antidote to all this fear and speculation is to recognize that what you truly are is outside time, unborn, and undying. You are the field in which birth, existence, and death appear.

It has been said by St. Francis and others that by dying you will realize eternal life. The Sufis say 'you must die before you die.' This dying is the death of the illusion of the separate and individual self. In the removal of the 'I,' death is deprived of its prey.

From the perspective of 'me,' this is an unsatisfactory answer to the life-after-death question. It says there is no life after death for the illusion you think you are, but the good news is that it also affirms that there is no death for that which you truly are.

Modern medical technology has allowed doctors to retrieve people from beyond the brink of what was once considered dead. Many of these people have reported near-death experiences (NDE's). In light of the available information, such experiences deserve to be taken seriously, but their actual meaning remains open to speculation. The interpretation of such reports is, of course, subjective and further complicated by the fact that they are often colored by the person's cultural background. Some people take them as proof of an afterlife, while others are very busy trying to explain them away.

In NDE's there often seems to be a perceived threshold, which the person having the experience considers a point of no return. From the perspective of this text, going beyond that threshold is simply the final step, after which one's individuality merges back into the oceanic Self. Admittedly, this seems to contradict the extensive research of Dr. Ian Stevenson. His books on reincarnation are well known, and he has investigated many cases, several of which make a very persuasive argument for this possibility.

However, even when we accept Dr Stevenson's case studies as authentic, it does not necessarily prove that individual souls engage in 'body hopping.' It is certainly conceivable that the one Self who plays all the roles can know of his act of Julius Caesar while playing the role of Robin Hood. In that case, it would not be Robin Hood who remembers a former life, but the universal actor knowing one of his other 'performances' while appearing *as* the character Robin Hood. This may more easily occur when there are quite a few similar 'building blocks' in the two characters. As such, it is not Julius Caesar *re*-incarnated, but the continuously incarnating one Self. This means that at the end of the show, the curtain falls for Robin Hood, but the actor remains unaffected.

Yet another way of looking at reincarnation is to see that this *as it is,* is all there is, and that this essential oneness, appearing as the totality of existence, includes the illusion of apparently separate people with memories of supposed past lives. We have to remember that these are still only metaphoric and linear descriptions of the essentially non-linear reality. They have been included here to show that evidence for reincarnation can be interpreted in multiple ways.

All this is not meant to say dead is dead and that is that. What has to be seen is that immortality does not mean perpetuating the mortal and that infinity is not an extension of the finite. In transcending the mortal and the finite, you'll find that you truly are beyond death; paradoxically to see this, one has to be willing to die. Like a rabbit in a noose, we trap ourselves with resistance. For the rabbit, as well as for us, the way out is the way in. In this dying we give up our sense of separation, which defines us as limited entities. To break out of this cocoon – to give up our limited sense of self – is what we fear the most, since it entails the eradication of 'me.' Given that entering Club Immortality requires that the sense of being an individual be left at the door, it's cold comfort to the ego that the door to eternal life is wide open

As always, we run into the paradox that if the ego is an illusion, 'I' cannot give it up. The concept of 'me' getting rid of my ego is as credible as a trap that has been set to catch itself. The ego seems to be clinging to life and to the idea of being an individual; but, in fact, the ego problem *is* the clinging itself. It's like learning to swim where any attempt to hold onto the water will lead to sinking. Letting go of the attempt to hold on dissipates the tension, and suddenly you'll find that you can stay afloat.

A joke is always much funnier when you get it yourself than when you need it to be explained. In the same way, this explaining away of the ego may not trigger a sudden surrender; but if the clinging is long and intense, there is a good chance of a sudden and spontaneous letting go. This letting go will make you laugh and see that it is so easy to relax, to let go of the hypnosis, and just be what you are. Words can make it seem difficult, but it is neither complex nor simple. It is the clear silent space, which exists prior to – and is forever unaffected by – such dualistic concepts. Once this is recognized, you'll see that birth, existence, and death do not happen *to* you, but *in* you.

For as long as you can remember, you have known the

body, the temporary aspect of the Self, and have thought of it as you. Now *be* the unity of the eternal and the temporal and *re*-cognize this as your true identity. Here is your invitation to give up the ghost right now in this very moment. Give up the illusion and realize that, in truth, you are already free of birth and dying.

You are one and the same
In joy and sorrow,
Hope and despair,
Life and death.
You are already fulfilled.
*Let yourself dissolve.**

* *The Heart of Awareness* (5-4) a translation of the Ashtavakra Gita by Thomas Byrom. Shambhala Publications

18

Blinded by the light

There is a story about a soldier who was sentenced to death. On the day of his execution, he is transported in an open cart to the gallows. As he takes in his surroundings for what he believes to be the last time, a great stillness descends upon him. The world appears in a clear and transparent vision of unity and harmony. His fear of dying is replaced with a deep sense of peace in which he and all of creation are one in a mystical union with God. At the very last moment, the king pardons the soldier. He regains his freedom and life, but loses the vision of paradise. The rest of his life is a hopeless quest to regain that vision. He takes to heavy drinking and dies years later as a lonely alcoholic.

For me the experience came when I was twenty-one. For several reasons, I felt at the end of my rope, and as it slipped through my fingers, my overwhelming sense of desperation suddenly lifted. *I've Got a Feeling* from the Beatles' album *Let It Be* was playing on the stereo, and it touched something deep inside of me. A large space opened up. It would be as true to say that I expanded to encompass the whole of existence as it would be to say that I had totally disappeared. Eternity, which I had understood as time without end, appeared as the absence of time. Everything was infused with life, including what, up until that moment, I had considered inanimate. All existence shared a common source and the first day of creation and the final day of destruction were seen as equally present. The Universe was neither big nor small. It revealed itself as simply One beyond all relative attributes, such as size, location, and time. While on the relative level, everything's purpose was shown to serve everything else in an intricate mosaic of perfect harmony, the totality of creation showed itself beyond purpose. I saw that it simply is as it is: Its own cause and fulfillment.

Things that really mattered before did not matter any longer. The people I saw from my window all seemed to be 'in the know' while pretending not to know who they really were. As the experience was slowing down, I remember thinking: *How can I go on with my day-to-day life, pretending to be this limited character? How can I go to work and face the daily routine again?* As it turned out, I was perfectly able to continue my life as before – but I was left with a certainty that, even when I do not see it, all is as it should be.

What the soldier's and my personal story have in common is that they show a vision of the eternal recounted as an experience with a beginning and an end. It has been called a mystical, transcendental or peak experience, and that is exactly what it is – an experience.

The content of such experiences seems to vary from person to person, depending on one's personality and socio-cultural background; but in essence, all peak experiences are similar in that they all recount a unity of man and God (or whatever name you're comfortable with), and they all transcend space and time. It is the sort of experience that people who want enlightenment are looking for; and many have confused it with enlightenment, as did I. What is generally overlooked, however, is the silent background in which both the experience and the 'I' that remembers and interprets it occur. To this mirror-like Awareness, such an experience is simply another cloud drifting by.

Over the years, that experience has been a source of both comfort and confusion to me. There was a clear memory of a vision of universal oneness, even though it was not always felt. My initial interpretation of the experience was that if all is One, then everybody and everything is part of this oneness. Later, I realized that this was a linguistic trap – that if all is truly One, there are no parts and there can be no you and me to be part of it. I saw that the 'I' of this body/mind is the same 'I' living in and as everybody else. Perhaps an apt analogy would be to say we are all the same Self dressed in a variety of costumes.

At the same time, there persisted this contradictory sense of being an individual entity responsible for my actions. Before I came to a simple and clear *'This is it*, I am *it*, and that is *that*,' this concept of being 'part of it' made me work on myself to be a better part. In the Hsin Hsin Ming, by Sengtan, the third Zen Patriarch, this working on the mind with the mind to make the 'good' victorious over the 'bad' is described, as follows:

> *If you want to get the plain truth,*
> *Be not concerned with right and wrong.*
> *The conflict between right and wrong*
> *Is the sickness of the mind.**

---

* From *The Way of Zen* by Alan Watts. Vintage

There was a continued interest in matters considered spiritual, as well as an interest in the parallels between the mystical experience and subjects like the new physics, the Gaia theory, and the ideas of an imminent evolutionary leap for humankind.

More recently, a renewed attraction to the non-dual teachings of Advaita, Taoism, and Zen emerged. It was like a revival of sorts, and I reread books like the Tao Te Ching, the Ashtavakra Gita, and the Way of Zen, as well as new books from Tony Parsons, Ramesh Balsekar, Nathan Gill, and many others. The same old words seemed to speak to me in a fresh and clear manner. It was like the missing pieces of a puzzle fell into place, and at the same time, it clearly showed that nothing could ever be out of place.

I met Wayne Liquorman during a seminar with his teacher Ramesh Balsekar. I told him that I was attending to experience the presence of people like him and Ramesh and that there were no questions I could ask, as I had a complete intellectual understanding of the material that was discussed. He answered, 'Yes but you still say *I* understand.' I did not respond much to this as I took it to be semantics; but somehow it stayed with me. It kept coming back to my mind, percolated down into my heart, and finally said, 'Actually there is no *'I'* that understands *it*. There is simply understanding.'

Presently 'I' remains as 'my address in life,' as well as a grammatical convention and convenience, which I will not hesitate to use. There is, however, no objective 'me' that can be identified or taken hold of. It is clear that my earlier mystical experience was not enlightenment. The idea of an 'I' having this experience created the confusing paradox of an 'I' having a non-dual experience. Now, it is obvious that the so-called mystical experience is as much an experience as having a glass of wine, making love, doing the shopping, or taking a walk in the rain. It is all just happening *as* me – not *to* or *by* me. The silent background in which experience appears and disappears had escaped the attention of the 'me' that thought he 'got it.'

Don't get me wrong: It is not that I didn't quite get it before and now I do. It is now clear that there is no 'I' to get it. The whole concept of someone getting enlightened has lost its validity. Enlightenment appears as a goal that one can reach only as long as there is the illusion of a separate entity or ego. In Zen, it has been called the *gateless gate*. When one stands before it, the gate seems to be there. When one passes through and looks back, it's clear there never was a gate, nor anyone to go through it.

The mystical experiences described above – both the condemned soldier's and mine – however attractive they may sound, were in the end a 'blinding by the light.' There is no need to have such experiences for understanding to happen. True understanding will level the artificial boundaries between the mystical and the mundane, the extraordinary and the ordinary, the experience and the one who experiences. It will reveal the splendor and the simplicity, along with the freedom – even from the need to be free – that lies beyond this apparent duality.

*There is a freedom –
even from the need to be free
even from the need to try to be spiritual.
This is beyond the duality of awake and asleep,
enlightened, and unenlightened.*

---

* From *How about Now?* by Arjuna. SelfXPress.

This is relaxation into the suchness of things
just the way things are.

This text points to absolute instead of relative and conditional freedom. Absolute freedom's inherent nature is such that there cannot be any conditions that have to be met before this freedom can be realized. There is no need for a special experience to set you free. When you wait for such an event, you feed the erroneous belief that there really is a 'you' in need of liberation. Such an anticipated event may be a transcendental experience; but even when you do get such an experience, it can become a trap instead of a liberation. The one having such an experience may be overwhelmed and conclude that this should become a permanent state.

There is a book by Suzanne Segal called *Collision with the Infinite*. It tells the story of a woman who got shocked by the sudden realization that there is no personal self. She was not a seeker and had no interest in things like yoga, Zen, and advaita. She thought she was losing her mind and sought help from psychiatrists and psychologists; but they were unable to help her. At some point, she came in contact with the non-dual perspective and from that point on, her situation started to improve – so much so that she started to hold meetings and began to help people on their spiritual path.

By the end of the book, she gets sick and dies. In the afterword her friend Stephan Bodian writes:

*Yet toward the end of her life, we could only watch as the realization slipped between her fingers like so much sand, leaving her frustrated and confused.**

---

* From *Collision with the Infinite* by Suzanne Segal. Blue Dove Press

Suzanne Segal was a unique case, and her situation involved a brain tumor; but in general, when *'the experience'* – like all experience – turns out to be impermanent, one might mistakenly consider this as a personal failing. Like the condemned soldier, one may end up chasing the experience, which is missing the point completely, much as one of the actors in the following story does:

Imagine watching a movie in which two men walk toward you. The setting is a desert. The sun is blazing overhead, and a huge mountain range is visible in the distance.

One of the men stops and says to his companion, 'Do you realize that this is all an illusion and we are just variations in one single light appearing as us, the sun, the sky, and the whole landscape?' His friend looks puzzled as he continues. 'This whole world we see is a flat screen, though it appears as if there is space all around us.'

Now his friend gets slightly worried. He thinks perhaps his buddy has been affected by the heat, so he asks, 'Are you feeling all right?'

'Absolutely fine! It is just suddenly obvious that all this is really nothing but a very clever illusion appearing on a single background.'

'Really,' says his friend getting slightly annoyed. 'Please show me this background.'

'Well look, here it is; right here touching us, carrying us. It contains everything we see.' He turns and points to the screen. His friend follows his finger, but sees nothing but the far off mountains.

If transcendental experiences arise on 'the screen' of Pure Awareness, so be it. If they do not, don't worry about it.

There are people who have had such experiences and are still seeking. There are also people who never had such an experience and are clear on what they truly are. Human experience is an ever-changing flow, but the clear space of Pure Awareness in which this flow occurs does not change. All there is is this presence, expressing itself as the totality of manifestation, including everything, from the most distant galaxy to smallest living creature, from the illusion of space and time to the way you appear as a character. This totality – both *what* arises and that *in which* it arises – is your true identity. There is absolutely nothing you can or have to do, nor is there anything you have to wait for to simply be what you already are.

> *Just sit there right now.*
> *Don't do a thing. Just rest.*
> *For your separation from God*
> *is the hardest work in the world.**

---

*From (Hafiz) *Love Poems from God: Twelve Sacred Voices from the East and West* translated by Daniel Ladinsky. Penguin Books

19

Concepts and metaphors

Before the final chapters, let us revisit some concepts and metaphors mentioned in this book. It gives us the opportunity to view them from different angles, while consistently pointing to the true Self and affirming that you are *it*. Some poems, quotes, and stories will be used to illustrate these concepts. If you want to play along, you are welcome; if you are not into this, just skip this chapter.

Once again, these concepts are not the truth, but they attempt to point at it, much like the fingertip attempting to touch itself, knowing that it cannot be done but, nevertheless, unwilling to stop trying.

Playing...
The 11th century Persian poet Omar Khayyam wrote:

> *For in and out, above, about below,*
> *'Tis nothing but a Magic Shadow Show,*
> *Played in a Box whose Candle is the Sun,*
> *Round which we Phantom*
> *Figures come and go.**

In this *Magic Shadow Show* there are no individuals. There

---
* From *The Rubaiyat of Omar Khayyam*

is only the Universal Puppeteer playing and animating all the characters – the One manifesting as the many; God playing hide and seek; the original energy animating this whole manifestation and pretending to be you, me, and everything else.

There seem to be other things than God, but only because he is dreaming them up and making them his disguises to play hide-and-seek with himself. The universe of seemingly separate things is therefore real only for a while, not eternally real, for it comes and goes as the Self hides and seeks itself.*

When a puppeteer gives a performance where a male and female doll – let's call them John and Kate – are having an argument, the audience sees two people arguing, while the puppeteer is hidden from sight. In reality, there is no life in these characters other than that of the puppeteer. The puppeteer simultaneously plays the male and the female roles and keeps the argument between them going. Although the characters express anger, the puppeteer is not angry. The invisible puppeteer is simultaneously both characters and neither one of them. We could imagine the following dialogue:

Kate: Why do we argue? The characters John and Kate do not even exist!
John: What are you talking about? Of course we exist. I can see you as clear as day.
Kate: We only appear to exist as separate entities. In

---

* From *The Book On The Taboo Against Knowing Who You Are* by Alan Watts. Vintage

fact, there is only One. And this One is both moving the illusory you *and* the illusory me.

John: This sounds like total nonsense, unless you know something that I don't.

Kate: There *is* no 'me' that knows something you don't.

John: Ah, you admit that you don't even know what you're talking about?

Kate: It is *that* in me playing the role of Kate that knows. It is the same energy that is playing you and pretending that you don't know.

John: So you're saying that I'm pretending?

Kate: No John, *I* don't say anything, but what is being said here is that neither you nor I exist. We're an illusion. *Something* is pretending to be you and me.

John: I'm sorry Kate, but I can't follow you. You're talking plain nonsense here. If we don't exist, how come we're having this conversation? I think you're trying to confuse me because you were losing the argument. Why don't we talk about things that *really matter, such as....*

Acting

The above is not meant to say that we are mere puppets. It says that we are *that* which appears *as* the puppets. To use another metaphor, you are the actor and not the role. Someone who sees his limited role or ego as reality is like a hypnotized actor playing a villain and becoming so absorbed in his play that he has forgotten who he really is. When he is released from the hypnotic illusion, he sees that the villain never existed. It would be incorrect to say that the villain has realized that he is, in fact, the actor. It is the actor who sees that he is not, nor ever was, the villain. Nothing will prevent him from continuing in his role, but he will no longer think of himself as the villain.

Telling a seeker that he is the Universal Actor (or IT) may lead him to draw the conclusion that he – John Doe – is IT. IT does appear as John Doe, but John Doe is not IT in the same way that the wave is an 'act' of the ocean, but the ocean not an 'act' of the wave. This reminds me of a story I heard as a child.

A philosopher (I forgot his name) was walking by the seashore pondering the mystery of God when he came upon a playing child. The child was using an undersized bucket to transfer water from the sea to a hole he had dug in the sand. The philosopher watched him for a while and finally asked what he was doing. 'I'm putting the sea in this hole,' was his answer.

The philosopher smiled. 'You'll never be able to fit the sea in there.'

The child paused and then said, 'It's more likely that I'll shift the ocean to this hole than that you'll succeed in fitting God's mystery into your head.'

To return to our metaphor, the actor can 'know' the John Doe character, but John Doe can never know the actor. The actor appearing as John Doe is the eternal, and remains the same whether he plays Julius Caesar, Mahatma Gandhi, Joan of Arc, or the girl behind the counter in the candy store. John Doe is the temporal role and has no existence apart from the actor.

This again says that you – as John Doe – can never 'get it' or become enlightened. You can never see *that which*

does the seeing; you're always *that which 'does' the being.*
Behind the illusion of being John Doe, enlightenment or
Self-realization already is.

> *There was a Door to which I found no Key:*
> *There was a Veil past which I could not see:*
> *Some little Talk awhile of Me and Thee There seem'd*
> *- and then no more of Thee and Me.**

On having a soul

Many who sense this animating energy call it their energy,
their soul or spirit, and believe it to be their individual and
personal essence instead of the universal and impersonal
energy. In reality, there is no one separate from this energy
to sense it. The energy itself is Self-aware and appearing as
the characters who believe that they are separate entities
with souls. As part of the play, they may sense eternal-
ness and believe they will live on after they die or will
reincarnate into a new life form. In a sense, they are right.
This essence is immortal and constantly incarnates in or as
new forms. The Self may in a current incarnation, as part
of the play, recall a 'previous life' and thus strengthen the
illusion of individuality. The thing to keep in mind is that
this vital energy is not a personal soul, but is the impersonal undivided Self, appearing as all there is, including
the character that has memories of a previous life.

We could call it the One Substance, the 'cosmic clay'
morphing into myriads of forms, such as mountains, stars,
and clouds, as well as your body/mind/heart organism;
complete with thoughts, feelings, emotions, and a sense of
volition and individuality. This One Substance constitutes

---

* From *The Rubaiyat of Omar Khayyam*

the essential nature of all that is. The shape it takes is inseparable from the substance itself; but the illusion may be so strong that we do not see through it. It can be like several beautiful statues making you forget the clay they were shaped from. The clay is the 'one soul' or common essence of the statues.

When it is clear that you are this One Substance, not just one of the temporal shapes it assumes, the belief in a personal 'me' with an individual soul drops away.

On and off

Another way to look at this essence or vital energy is as the one source of all apparent opposites including the non-manifested and manifested universe. Both the manifest and non-manifest appear in and arise out of this singularity. It is the One that knows no second, the ultimate subject that cannot be objectified or made into a concept. As the non-manifest, it could be said to be at rest. With a big bang – or through a Genesis scenario – marking the beginning of time, it becomes the manifest and could be said to be in action.

As perceived from the human perspective, the cosmic drama is played out between the interdependent polar opposites of here/there, up/down, you/me, good/evil, birth/death, etc.

> *Under heaven all can see beauty as beauty*
> *only because there is ugliness.*
> *All can know good as good because there is evil.**

---

* From *Tao Te Ching* translated by Gia-Fu Feng and Jane English. Wildwood House Ltd.

Or the following:

> *All creation, from this perch, is made from this incredible*
> *foundation. Every mountain, every star, the smallest*
> *salamander or woodland tick, each thought in our mind,*
> *each flight of a ball is but a web of elemental yes/nos*
> *woven together.**

The above words seem to come from a mystical textbook, but are, in fact, from an article on computation in Wired Magazine. Alan Watts termed it the Zero One amazement, while Freud saw the same pattern but interpreted it as something derived from and pointing to sexuality. I wonder if he missed the point that all yeses and nos, ins and outs, ups and downs – including sexual ins and outs and ups and downs – are the same basic rhythm through which the underlying unity expresses itself.

This apparent duality is vital to the game of manifestation, much like the black and white pieces are essential to the game of chess. Black and white oppose each other on one level and form a single game at another level.

Just as electricity comes in positive and negative particles that activate all kinds of toys, tools, and gadgets, the one Self activates/plays all there is, including the myriad of characters totally absorbed in their roles as apparently separate individuals. Traditionally, the universal actor chooses to play the game of awakening and knowing itself in relatively few characters. This, however, may be changing. It seems that 'the veil is thinning,' that awakening is being demystified, and more and more ordinary

---

* *God is the Machine* by Kevin Kelly. Wired Magazine, December 2002.

people, just like you and me, are recognizing what they truly are.

The metaphor of electricity
In comparing this animating force to electricity and likening body-mind organisms to appliances, we get an interesting analogy. This story also contains a pointer as to what happens when the body dies.

Electricity has always existed as potential energy, but to manifest, electricity needs a medium, be it a thunderstorm or a steam iron. There are countless electric appliances doing different things; from mixing fruit to making phone calls, from navigating space shuttles to playing movies, from setting off explosives to monitoring vital signs in intensive care units around the world. Notwithstanding this wide variety of activities, all these appliances are powered (enlivened, if you will) by the same energy. When a fruit mixer breaks down, nothing happens to the electricity. That which animated the now broken machine is itself unbroken.

The impersonal energy animating the human apparatus *also generates the thoughts* with which this apparatus thinks of itself as the responsible source of its activity. In other words, this *sense* of 'me' as a person with volition and responsibility is, in fact, an *activity* of this impersonal animating energy. It is the deep Self playing the melody of *I am so and so doing this and that* on the instruments of countless body-mind organisms. It is the illusion of multiplicity, the grand dance of creation and destruction manifesting in a timeless presence – essentially a one-man band.

With Earth's first Clay They did the Last Man's knead,
And then of the Last Harvest sow'd the Seed:
Yea, the first morning of creation wrote
What the last dawn of reckoning shall read.*

Come join the dance

It is, of course, a sad situation when we find ourselves dancing just to reach the end of a dance. In its purest form, dancing is movement for its own sake and does not have a destination. It has no other reason for being, other than its expression in the present moment. The purposeless essence of dancing is an often-used metaphor for life or the way it is lived, as here in a poem by Rumi.

Dance, when you're broken open.
Dance, if you've torn the bandage off.
Dance in the middle of the fighting.
Dance in your blood.
Dance, when you're perfectly free.**

The Divine, appearing as the dance of life, is known in India as Leela. Leela is the Self at play through the dynamic rhythm that finds expression in the act of creation. It expresses as this multi-faceted manifestation, from the stately rotating galaxies deep in outer space to the rapidly spinning particles at the subatomic level; from the Earth's trajectory around the sun to the vital activity in the cells of our bodies; from the soaring flight of the eagle to the moth flitting at the candle's flame.

---

* From *The Rubaiyat of Omar Khayyam*
** From *The Essential Rumi* compiled and translated by Coleman Barks. Castle Books

This vibrant, pulsating display of energy has no purpose beyond itself, and in this very purposelessness lies its infinite delight. To the one hearing this music, it extends an open invitation to realize the ever-present flow that is going on, to simply go with it and surrender to its causeless joy. When this invitation is accepted, it becomes plain as the nose on your face that any step taken to get closer to one's true Self is one step too many. In the surrender to this 'trip the light fantastic,' life leads; and every step is from the Self and by the Self. Here, the borders between the dancers blur and dissolve until only the dance remains. The journey is the destination, and all is happening of its own accord. One is forever starting afresh and forever arriving at the warm intimacy of one's true home. The free person who feels this rhythm simply happens, just like the stars, the space, the sounds, and the silence.

> *...where past and future are gathered.*
> *Neither movement from nor towards,*
> *Neither ascent nor decline.*
> *Except for the point, the still point,*
> *There would be no dance,*
> *And there is only the dance.**

About silence, nothingness and the heart

To talk about silence seems a paradox, as the sound of one's words apparently shatters the silence. Most of us have learned that silence is the polar opposite of sound and that sound can break it; but understanding this differently, we find that silence is to the ear what space is to the eye. When an object is perceived in space, we do not think that space

---

* T.S. Eliot (1888-1965)

has been broken. In the same way when sound appears in silence, silence has not been broken. Silence contains sound in the same way that space contains objects. When you notice this, each sound is surrounded by silence.

Space and silence are both great pointers to – and arise in – what is even more subtle: the silent space of Pure Awareness. The eye of the cyclone or the heart of the storm is silent. It's like the empty space at the center of a wheel. Seen in this light, emptiness is a potent no-thing-ness; it is that around which the storm revolves and that which allows the wheel to turn around its axel. Or consider the empty heart of a flute, which supplies the resonant space for its tones. This can again be a pointer to the creative emptiness of Pure Awareness, which allows for this whole manifestation to arise.

> *Thirty spokes share the wheel's hub;*
> *It is the center hole that makes it useful.*
> *Shape clay into a vessel;*
> *It is the space within that makes it useful.*
> *Cut doors and windows for a room;*
> *It is the holes which make it useful.**

When we try to fathom the living emptiness at our very center, we cannot find its end or edge. It is beyond all dualistic qualifications. It is our true heart and at the same time all around us.

In discussing the heart, we often mean the seat of emotion/intuition as opposed or complementary to the intellect. What is important here is see that both the

---

* From *Tao Te Ching* translated by Gia-Fu Feng and Jane English. Wildwood House Ltd.

emotions *and* the intellect arise from the same single source. We could refer to this as the heart of hearts, the central and true core of being-ness; an absolute and still no-thing-ness, which escapes each and every attempt to grasp it with the mind.

See for yourself how absolutely impossible it is to form an idea of this no-thing-ness. Every idea about it is *some*-thing and therefore not *no*-thing. When the intellect tries to imagine this, it comes to a screeching halt. This no-thing-ness is an impenetrable brick wall for the mind; but for no-mind it is a warm bath, a coming home to the heart of hearts.

Back to basics
All the seeking, all the spiritual practices, and all the effort to understand veils the plain and simple truth of *this, as it is*. Whatever thought arises, whatever feeling comes up, be it labeled good or bad, there is something still and quietly aware of all that's going on. It simply is, without the slightest effort. Snap your fingers. Did you hear the sound? How much effort did that take? None! Now, at this very moment, Pure Awareness is the silent background to you reading these words. You don't have to do a thing for it to be there. It is always present, even though it is too close to get at, like the eye is too close to see itself.

This silent space of Pure Awareness is not what we call attention. Attention wanders from place to place. In a matter of seconds it darts from the words on the page to the itch on the arm to the memory of last night's lovemaking to thoughts about needing to pay that bill and back to the page. The flitting motion of your attention happens within Pure Awareness. Attention moves, but Pure Awareness remains unmovable. Wherever you are – in your deep sleep, in your dreams, and in all the fluctuations of your waking state – Pure Awareness is. Your body, your car, and the dog are all manifestations in and of Pure Awareness. In all its variety, it remains One.

There is no judgment in Pure Awareness. It is not about being good or bad, right or wrong, peaceful or upset. It allows all this to arise, and sees it all fade away again. When time runs out and the manifested universe dissolves, Pure Awareness still is.

To let go and relax into (or *as*) Pure Awareness is the most natural thing in the world. No effort, no trying, no seeking is needed; but if you want to make an effort or want to seek a little more, it is perfectly all right. Whether you stress and strain or become very quiet, Pure Awareness reflects it all without the slightest effort or judgment.

> *Sitting quietly*
> *Doing nothing*
> *Spring comes*
> *And the grass grows by itself* *

Limits of language

When reading on the subject of non-duality, one may find diametrically opposed statements, concepts, and metaphors in different books or even in the same book.

For instance:

- You are IT/ You don't exist;
- The ultimate understanding/There is nothing to understand;

---

* Matsuo Basho (1644-1694) Zen poet and father of the Haiku genre of poetry.

- Enlightenment/There is no enlightenment;
- Everything is IT/Everything is just an illusion;
- There is only the Self (Advaita)/There is no Self (Buddhism).

This shows that it is basically impossible to say something about Self-realization without running into seeming contradictions. Whatever we say about it is as true or untrue as its opposite. We can try to negate the problem of capturing the non-dual and non-linear in dualistic and linear word strings by using metaphors and parables and by pointing out that they are merely concepts; but we will still not succeed in kissing our own lips.

Take for example a simple sentence like 'Pure Awareness is beyond all concepts.' Labeling Pure Awareness as *being beyond concepts* objectifies it as a new concept. The Hindus point at what cannot be spoken by calling it *Neti Neti*: Not this, Not this, or neither this nor that. To the Hebrews it's Yod-He-Vau-He, the unspeakable name of God. No matter how we try, by talking or thinking about this we cannot escape the limitation of making *it* into a concept, and so *it* forever escapes each and every attempt to define *it*. *It* remains forever a paradoxical and intimate mystery, an ongoing open question, and a constant answer.

Even when speaking of matters that are suitable for the linear and dualistic medium of language, it is simply impossible to know the different interpretations people give to certain words or how they will understand what is being communicated. (The movie 'Being There' with Peter Sellers uses this type of confusion to tell a great story.)

The apparently contradictory concepts mentioned above are all pointers to your true Self and, as such, are neither factual nor fictional. Rather, they are like different little stones thrown against your bedroom window. When you hear them, you may get out of bed, look outside, and be surprised to see your lover there. Would it matter which exact pebble was the one that woke you?

20

The dream of space and time

Time is what is indicated by a clock.

Albert Einstein 1879-1955

'When you are courting a nice girl an hour seems like a second. When you sit on a red-hot cinder a second seems like an hour. That's relativity.'

Albert Einstein 1879-1955

In our dreams we may encounter age-old mountains, oceans, stars, and planets. There may be people and animals, cities and forests. We may experience days or even years passing by. To the dreamer, it is all very real. The dreamer may run from an erupting volcano, and the accompanying fear can be so intense that it jolts him awake, at which point he is no longer concerned with what happened to the volcano or the other objects and characters that just moments ago populated his universe. From the perspective of the waking state, the dream may have lasted only a few seconds. Where was the time, the space, and the objects that filled it? We can say it was inside the dreamer, but it's equally true to say that the dreamer was inside the dream. This common experience clearly shows how apparently solid realities such as the world of objects, space, and time could well be illusory in nature.

> *...there is evidence to suggest that our world and every-thing in it – from snowflakes to maple trees to falling stars and spinning electrons – are also only ghostly images, projections from a level of reality so beyond our own it is literally beyond both space and time.**

In the 'real world,' space and time constitute relative spatial and temporal relationships between so-called objects and events, as well as between the observer and the observed. There are no absolutes from this perspective, which reminds me of William Blake's words:

> *To see a World in a Grain of Sand*
> *And a Heaven in a Wild Flower,*
> *Hold Infinity in the palm of your hand*
> *And Eternity in an hour.***

The human being appears here as a reference point from which events may be perceived as occurring in the past or the future. Objects appear to be older or younger or bigger or smaller than the observer. They seem to be moving fast or slowly or to be located far from or close to the observer. In one direction, space stretches outwards endlessly and contains relatively huge objects; while in the other direction, the infinitely small balances the scale. Man always occupies the place between these extremes. What's more, man's relative position and observations are the touchstone

---

* From *The Holographic Universe* by Michael Talbot. Harper Collins
** From *Auguries Of Innocence*. Original Text: William Blake, *Poems*, ed. Dante Gabriel Rossetti (1863)

without which the two sides simply would not manifest.

Let's get back to the dream with the erupting volcano. The dreamer contains the dream and, at the same time, occupies a relative position in the dream. Everything in his dream, whether rocks or clouds, feelings or thoughts, people or animals, is made of 'dream stuff,' and as the dreamed character, he can say:

Like the shadow
I am
and
I am not*

Now consider the possibility that the Self dreams up this manifestation in a similar way. Like the dreamer appearing in his own dream, we can say that the Creator appears in his manifestation while, at the same time, the manifestation appears in the Creator. Dreamlike, He manifests the whole cosmic drama out of Himself.

He is hidden in His manifestation, manifest in His concealing.
He is outward and inward, near and far...**

The substance of this dreamed up 'reality' is Pure Awareness – *the dream that stuff is made of.* In this reality/dream the mind appears and superimposes on this undivided whole the illusion of separate objects and events by inventing boundaries in space and time.

---

* *The Love Poems of Rumi* edited by Deepak Chopra. Harmony Books
** *Doctrine of the Sufis* by Muhammed Al-Kalabadhi translated by Arthur John Arberry AMS Press

Let me ask you a question. Where did the event of 'you' have its beginning? Was it at birth, at conception, or when your grandparents' grandparents met? No matter where you draw the line, it will be arbitrary and defines an artificial boundary. In the game of day-to-day living, these conceptual borders come in handy; but most of us have long forgotten that they are entirely conceptual.

Awareness is Self-luminous and does not need to be aware of anything outside itself. In other words, Awareness is all there is. In the universal dream, just as in the dreams we have at night, there is the illusion of this and that, near and far, past and future, self and other, which creates the relative experiences of space and time – but space and time in and of themselves have no reality. The 'mind-generated objects' in this universe are temporal occurrences and only have size and form relative to each other. Ultimately, however, there are no distinct objects or events separated by space and time, nor does the dream itself have a fixed size or time span. The dream and the dreamer are one-and-the-same Self-aware reality.

> *Plop, there it is!*
> *Nothing else than that, which is empty of matter, fills all corners of the universe!*
> *Mountains, rivers, the entire world, you and all, they manifest the body of the*
> *One.*[*]

You, as a dream character, are a temporary occurrence, while you as the dreamer are beyond space and time. When you wake up to this realization, you will be as unconcerned

---

[*] Buddhist poem

with your personal story as you are with the character you appeared to be in your dream.

This is not to say that you will be indifferent and without feelings. When reading a good novel, you are aware of its illusory nature, but nevertheless become engrossed in the characters and unfolding plot. In the same way, as long as you appear as a dreamed character, you will not wake up from the dream, but you might awaken *to* the dream.

21
Awakening to the dream

Lucid dreaming is a term that refers to waking up inside a dream, realizing it is a dream, and then continuing the dream with this understanding. Seeing through the illusion of separation could be termed lucid living, as it is not you waking up *from* the dream of life, but the impersonal awakening *to* the dream of life. From which point could an illusion see through itself as an illusion? What could an assumed doer do to become a non-doer? What thought could take the thinker beyond thinking? The answer is nothing and none. Like Rumi said,

> *Whoever brought me here*
> *will have to take me home.*

This 'coming home' reveals the illusory nature of the ego, the world, time and space. All this does not disappear in a blast of white light, but what does disappear is the sense of separation that constitutes the ego illusion. Although it may put a glint in 'your' eye as 'you' delight in this cosmic illusion, there will be actually no you to delight in it, no you to see it, and no you to get it. The play, including your role in it, continues with the altered perspective of knowing, delighting, and seeing, without an individual claiming these as personal activities or achievements. What is left is *that* which appears *as* you and everything – your true Self, which is already and always awake to the dream of life.

This realization happens by itself. No new knowledge is acquired, but old assumptions fall away. No effort in the world can make you what you already and actually are. The truth behind ego is a no-thing-ness too close for investigation, since it is the very source from which the attempt to investigate arises. Seeing this makes it clear that the activating agent in all your actions is not a fictional 'me,' but the universal energy, or one's true Self. The belief in a 'me,' as well as the seeking for enlightenment, is seen through by no-one as nothing but the playful activity of this primal activating energy. The cosmic joke in the journey of the seeker is that the energy that fuels the seeking is precisely what is being sought. In Zen this is called 'riding an ox in search of an ox.' Wei Wu Wei compared it to looking for your spectacles, not realizing that they are on your nose and, were you not looking through them, you wouldn't be able to see what you are looking for.

IT awakens to itself or, more to the point, IT *is* Awakeness itself. It is the light in which all apparent opposites reveal their interdependence and ultimate One-ness; it is the clarity in which the illusion of separation dissolves. The witness and that which is witnessed merge into witnessing, while the illusion of past and future dissolves into the clarity of timeless presence. *As It Is,* life has no meaning beyond itself. It is always at the point of completion and, simultaneously, as fresh as the morning dew at the dawn of creation.

This Awakeness does not deliver a permanent transcendental state. The belief that awakening is about such a state – that it is an experience for someone – constitutes the enlightenment myth. It continues the illusion of a separate seeker and keeps you trapped in the search for the desired awakening.

That which you truly are *is* forever awake and present, not just in the extraordinary, but also in and as the ordinary. It is beyond simple and complex. It is the source of both. We could use the theories from quantum mechanics and theoretical physics to point at it, or we could use a nursery rhyme like:

Row, row, row your boat
Gently down the stream
Merrily, merrily, merrily, merrily
Life is but a dream.

Or the following:

Where did you come from, baby dear?
Out of Everywhere into here.

Chuck Hillig points at it in a wonderfully simple book *Enlightenment for Beginners,* and Wei Wu Wei dazzles the reader with his intellectual acrobatics, while pointing at the very same essence. Like clear water, it slips through the net of our concepts. It is smaller than the smallest and greater than the greatest; it is unborn, eternal, and forever free. It is simply One, expressing and manifesting itself as the complex illusion of the multitude that is the dance of creation.

To see that you are *this* is to remember what ultimately was never forgotten. It is a homecoming after a journey in fantasyland, a return to the place you never really left. It is the mystery that cannot be comprehended, but is recognized as *that which you already intimately are* – the silent background in and from which time, space, being, and non-being arise. It is the true Self, that which has no opposite, The One without a second, or Pure Awareness.

That was a dream,' God smiled and said,
'A dream that seemed to be true.
There were no people, living or dead,
there was no earth, and no sky o'er head:
there was only Myself – in you.*

* Ella Wheeler Wilcox, American writer and poet (1855-1919)

Afterword

I've told you all that constitutes the very core of Truth;
   There is no you, no me, no superior being, no disciple,
and no Guru.*

Perhaps this text has been nourishing, but if you consider yourself still hungry, here are some finishing words to chew on.

Many seekers have been around the spiritual block more than once without coming to an eagerly anticipated 'awakening.' Several believe that they have reached a complete intellectual understanding, but, nevertheless, they are still waiting for an event that proves to them that they are already fully awake. What is apparently not clear to them is that there is no one to have a complete intellectual understanding; that there simply is understanding and that wakefulness is already fully present. What stops them from seeing this is the false belief that there is indeed a separate individual that needs to have certain experiences to reach a so-called awakening. This Awakeness is not about someone having experiences, states of mind, or knowledge, but about seeing that there is no separate someone. It is about the undivided essence that is aware

---

* *Dattatreya's Song of the Avadhut.* Atma Books

of – and appears as – this whole universe, including the idea of a character that wants to have the experience of awakening. Pure Awareness is already fully present, so why not simply identify as Pure Awareness instead of as the character that's looking for confirmation?

When, in spite of intense practice, various teachers, numerous Satsangs, and all the right books, the seeking does not come to rest, it may help to see the 'connections.' From our unique vantage point in time, we can see relations and similarities between the different teachings, books, and scriptures that have been handed down through history. This 'overview' has not always been available. Did Jesus know of Buddha? Did Meister Eckhart know about Lao Tzu? Was Rumi familiar with Bodhidharma? Perhaps, but most likely they were not. Voices come to us from different cultures, from east and west, north and south, some centuries apart, yet all pointing in the same direction and sometimes literally saying the same things. Here are a few concrete examples:

Christianity: *For behold, the kingdom of God is within you. (Luke 17:21)*
Buddhism: *You are all Buddhas. There is nothing you need to achieve.*
Just open your eyes. (Siddhartha Gautama)
Zen: *If you cannot find the truth right where you are where else do you expect to find it? (Dogen Zenji)*
Taoism: *Great knowledge sees all in one. Small knowledge breaks down into the many. (Chuang Tzu)*
Science: *Bell's theorem demonstrates that the universe is fundamentally interconnected, interdependent, and inseparable.' (Fritjof Capra)*

Tibetan Buddhism: *There is not a single state that is not this vast state of presence.**
Islam: *'In that glory is no 'I' or 'We' or 'Thou.' 'I,' 'We,' 'Thou,' and 'He' are all one thing.'(Hallaj)*
Hinduism: *Tat Tvam Asi – Thou Art That.*
Judaism: *I am That I am.*

Is it not utterly fascinating that the same expressions are repeated over and over? Is it not heartening that they consistently point to the fact that all is one, that this is IT, and that you are IT ? Is this moment not the perfect moment to accept what they offer, to realize that it is your own voice inviting you home? If not *now*, then *when?*

It's not difficult to discover your Buddha Mind
But just don't try to search for it.
Cease accepting and rejecting possible places
Where you think it can be found
And it will appear before you**

I have heard people ask questions about the nature of enlightenment and then dismiss the answer by saying something like, 'These are just words and concepts. I have heard them before, and this is not enough. I want to know what it really is all about.' What such seekers are waiting for is a confirmation through a special event, or perhaps a peak experience, thus postponing the realization that the Awakeness they're looking for is already fully present. What they overlook is the actuality of *that* which does

---

* *Hsin Hsin Ming – verses on the faith mind* by Sengstan, 3rd Zen Patriarch. Produced by the Zen Buddhist Order of Hsu Yun

** *You Are the Eyes of the World* by Longchenpa. Snow Lion Publications

the seeing – that which everything has in common – the one universal canvas sustaining all manifestation. It is the substratum underlying all apparent diversity. It is the extraordinary in the absolutely ordinary. It is the common ground. Interestingly, common means both 'ordinary' as well as 'universal.' This common essence is our true nature, regardless of the shapes and diversity the mind projects on this undivided whole. It is the light that shines on everything, but cannot and needs not shine on itself. It is the magical illusion, the marvel that can manifest unity as diversity and the single as the many. It is the one identity or Pure Awareness.

> *The largest equals the smallest.*
> *There are no boundaries, no within and without.*
> *What is and what is not are the same,*
> *For what is not is equal to what is.*
> *If you do not awaken to this truth,*
> *do not worry yourself about it.*
> *Just believe that your Buddha Mind is not divided,*
> *That it accepts all without judgment.*
> *Give no thoughts to words and speeches or pretty plans*
> *The eternal has no present, past or future.**

The truth is, of course, not in these words but in the understanding of them. If you really hear, you're really here, and you encounter the answer everywhere. It is repeated in and as everything and says again and again, 'All is One. This is IT. You are IT.'

When all this is not enough, you'll probably follow your

---

* *Hsin Hsin Ming – verses on the faith mind* by Sengstan, 3rd Zen Patriarch. Produced by the Zen Buddhist Order of Hsu Yun

doubting mind around the block a few more times; but if you don't want to go that way once again, you might come to accept that these voices you know so well are actually right. They all affirm that you truly are the clear open space beyond all phenomena. They invite you to turn around a hundred and eighty degrees and to look directly to the place from where the looking arises, to remember the seeing, instead of merely emphasizing the scene. See, it is *always* the way it is. Even if you think you cannot accept *this as it is*, you'll find it impossible to reject it. *This*, as it is, before acceptance or rejection, before words and thoughts solidifying into concepts, is the actuality of being. It is limitless present Awareness. You are that spaciousness, containing absolutely everything, including the way you appear to yourself, complete with certainties, doubts, pains, pleasures and a possible sense of separation.

If no answer or concept can jolt you from your sense of separation, if you have reached a dead end in your search, perhaps it is possible to disregard all concepts, to simply surrender to *what is* and stand naked and alone as *this*. Perhaps you can stop waiting for an event to confirm that you are fully awake and simply accept that it *must be* already so. To accept that there is no separate you, and therefore no one in need of waking up, is a shortcut. You might call it the final 'stepless step.' Rip off all the labels, ignore the ever-changing stories in your head, and see what remains unchanged.

Stop imagining yourself being or doing this or that and the realization that you are the source and heart of all will dawn on you.

Sri Nisargadatta Maharaj

Sri Nisargadatta, when asked how he went 'beyond,' answered that his Guru told him that he was the supreme reality. The next question was what he did about it. 'I trusted him and remembered it,' was his answer.

When all this is clear, but there still is an ongoing belief in a separate you as the primal reality, then, once again, see directly who or what is aware of this apparent separation.

> *There is no greater mystery than this, that we keep seeking reality though in fact we are reality. We think that there is something hiding reality and that this must be destroyed before reality is gained. How ridiculous!*
>
> Ramana Maharshi

As we come to the end of this text, I wish you the courage to trust your Self and to identify as Pure Awareness instead of losing yourself in its content. This, as it is, is the ongoing invitation to shake off your imaginary shackles of separation and stand in freedom and clarity now.

Clarity is the term Nathan Gill uses to describe the falling away of seeking and the recognition of what you truly are. For the ripe seeker who actually already knows this but hesitates at the door, he wrote a small book called – you guessed it – *Clarity*. I'd like to end this book with the final words from *Clarity*:

> *Right now you are Consciousness, appearing as a character in your play.*
> *Maybe you think you need confirmation. Forget it. Relax. You already are That.*
> *With much love to You from Yourself.*

Selected Bibliography

Arberry, A.J. (trans). Doctrine of the Sufis. 1979. Cambridge University Press

Balsekar, R. Sin And Guilt. 2005. Zen Publications

Barks, C., Moyne, J. and Arberry, A.J. The Essential Rumi. 1994. Penguin Books

Byrom, T (trans). The Heart of Awareness. 1990. Shambhala Publications

Bohm. D. Wholeness and the Implicate Order. 1981. Routledge & Kegan Paul

Chopra, D. The Love Poems of Rumi. 1998. Random House

Drucker, A. (ed). Self-Realization. 1993. Sai Towers Publishing

Feng, G. and English, J. (trans) Tao Te Ching. 1972. Wildwood House Ltd.

Fitzgerald, E. The Rubaiyat of Omar Khayyam

Frydman, M. (ed). I Am That. 1973. Chetana Publications

Gill, N. Already Awake. 2004. Non-Duality Press

Godman, D. The Power of the Presence. 2000. David Godman

Guillaumont, A. The Gospel According to Thomas 1959. Harper & Row

Hillig, C. Enlightenment for Beginners. 1999. Black Dot Publications

Ladinsky, D. Love Poems from God. 2002. Penguin Books

Lewin, R. In the Age of Mankind. 1988. Smithsonian Institution

Liquorman, W. Acceptance of What Is. 2000. Advaita Press

Longchenpa. You Are the Eyes of the World. 2000. Snow Lion Publications.

Loy, D. Nonduality: A Study in Comparative Philosophy. 1997. Humanity Books

Menon, Sri Atmananda Krisna. Atma Darshan. 1946. Sri Vidya Samiti

Norbu, Chogyal Namkhai. Dzogchen: The Self-Perfected State. 2000 Snow Lion Publications

Parsons, T. As It Is. 2000. Inner Directions Publishing

Prasad, Dr. R. (trans) The Bhagavad-Gita. 1988. American Gita Society

Rossetti, D.G. (Ed.), William Blake, Poems, 1863.

Talbot, M. The Holographic Universe. 1992. Harper Collins

Waddell, N. The Unborn: The Life and Teachings of Zen Master Bankei. 2000. North Point Press

Watts, A. The Way of Zen. 1999. Vintage

Wei Wu Wei. Posthumous Pieces. 2004. Sentient Publications

Wei Wu Wei. Fingers Pointing Towards the Moon. 2003. Sentient Publications

Wei Wu Wei. Why Lazurus Laughed. 2004. Sentient Publications

Whitman, W. Song Of Myself

LaVergne, TN USA
25 August 2010
194581LV00001B/22/P